Bones Washed

in

Water and Wine

BY SYDNEY MARANGOU-WHITE

ISBN:

Paperback: 978-1470104801

Printer: CreateSpace
Cover Design: Chautona Havig, CanAm Author Services, LLC
Layout Design: CanAm Author Services, LLC

Fonts: Garamond, Trajan Pro, and Dumbldor

For my daughters: Helen (Mirabai) and Alexia.
And for my grandchildren: Cosmo and Millie, Cara, Daniel and
Jonathan

It was the best of times; it was the worst of times.

Charles Dickens
A Tale of Two Cities, 1859

Prosphorion,
Erissos,
Chalkidiki,
Greece,
January 8th, 1954.

Dear Sydney,

Owing to a lot of bad weather lately, and no doubt crowded mails, we had no word from you until yesterday, and then the postman brought your presents and your letter. Many thanks for the presents. The socks are going to be most useful, and your Godmother wants me to thank you very much for what you sent her. Your letter could hardly have contained better news, and was like another Christmas present to me. You seem to be getting along really well, and all the credit is due to your efforts. You must be very happy at starting your third year this month, and perhaps you will be getting your diploma for General Nursing within the next twelve months. Try and pass out as high as you can without getting brain fever from your efforts. But also see that you have a good time during this coming year; for life is meant to be enjoyed. You have made up all your lost time through having difficulties at the start of your education.

This last year has been a more fortunate one for the village. There were good rains at the right time, and they brought a good harvest, and on top of that we have had the best olive crop for several years. The olive mills were working up to Christmas, and there is still a little work for two of them. The Quakers sent out some new water-pipes, and so water is laid on to the village again; but only as far as the reservoir near the school, and the village will have to do the rest of the work inside the village. I think there have been fewer sick people than usual, though of course the winter is far from at an end. Unfortunately your grandfather has been in bed for some weeks now, and gets better very slowly. He gets up now two or three times in the day. Your father is still in the village but I think expects to go to Salonika in a few days, to do some work at the Quaker Girls' School.

We received a present of many bottles of vitamin drops from America, and have been dosing many weak people with them in the village, with good results. A very nice doctor comes to the village now, once a week, and everybody seems to like him. He is away at present, as he has gone to get married. Many pigs were killed at Christmas, and you cannot imagine how many presents we received of pieces of pork; we shall be eating salt and pickled pork for the rest of winter. In addition we were given bottles and bottles of wine, and a great deal of olive oil. The villagers here really have been generous to us.

Well, write again when you have time, and tell us how you like your new lectures. You must have a good deal of hospital experience behind you now. We gave your grandfather your latest news when we went to see him yesterday.

Very best New Year wishes.

Your affectionate Godfather,

Sydney Loch.

Acknowledgements

This book could not have been written without the encouragement and support of my family: I wish to thank especially my daughter Helen for finding me an editor-in-chief in Darcie Torres from the USA.

Many thanks are due to my numerous friends, in particular the "Oxton Lot".

I am also very grateful to Mark Ball who gave me editorial guidance and support, and especially to Karen Gleave for her constant encouragement and practical help throughout my venture in writing my autobiography, also to Kim Zadow for scanning the photographs and to Maureen Zadow for proofreading the manuscript.

Thanks are also due to John White for the map of Halkidiki, and to Cara for the family tree and editing of photographs.

Table of Contents

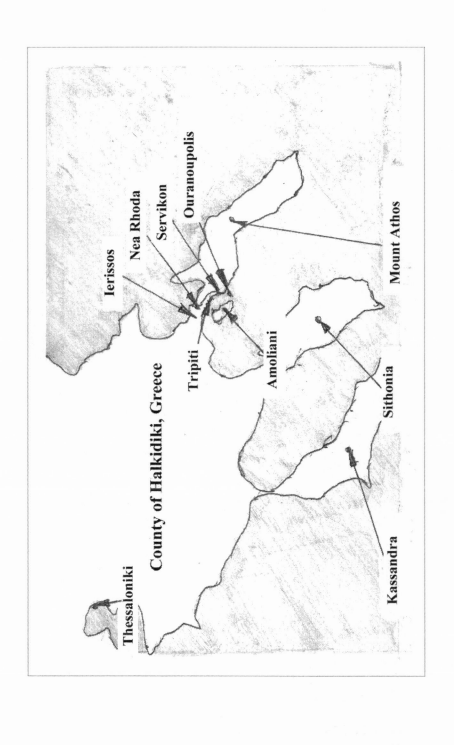

County of Halkidiki, Greece

Thessaloniki

Ierissos

Nea Rhoda

Servikon

Ouranoupolis

Tripiti

Amoliani

Mount Athos

Sithonia

Kassandra

Foreword

From Homer on, when has Greece been anything less than a
fascination? This account of a Greek childhood, in which I have
been privileged to have a very small hand in the editing, speaks of
northern Greece in the years before and surrounding the Second
World War, but is in many ways a most remarkable point of access
to a far older world, to a village Greece now almost lost beyond
recall, and a peasant Greece, both harsh and lyrical, that Homer
might well recognise. Sydney White had a long and distinguished
career in the British National Health Service, but few of her
colleagues could have guessed the world from which she came, nor
the difficulties that she had overcome. This is a family memoir,
written with directness and a natural grace, but it is also a historical
document, a testimony to Sydney's great character and courage, and
a unique view, by turns charming and alarming, into a Greece now
entirely beyond our reach.

Mark Ball MA (Cantab)
February 2010

In Retrospect

A eucalyptus tree marks her grave. It has a slender trunk and luxurious foliage, just like our mother when not pinned down by an attack of bronchial asthma.

My heart is heavy and my soul is sorrowful because today is the 26th of September, 1999. In nine days, on the 5th of October, my mother will have been buried in this grave for 31 years under the eucalyptus tree that was planted by my eldest brother, Byron.

It is the custom here in my little village in Greece to lift the bones after three years. However, Byron's resistance could simply not be breached; that is, until the cemetery was entirely full and we had no option but to comply with the law of the land. For my part, I wanted to disinter the bones of my parents, especially the bones of my dear mother. She died and was buried, but I was not at her funeral. I didn't know of her death until two weeks later. Thus, I wanted to see her to say goodbye: to take my leave from her and ask her to forgive me. I imagined that, somehow, if I could just see her bones, it would be like being present at my mother's funeral. Of course, it was not. It was anything but.

On that September day, it was like high summer: a clear blue sky dominated by such a fierce, blistering sun. My two brothers and I, employing the assistance of two Albanians, met at the cemetery at eleven o'clock in the morning. My sister could not be persuaded to accompany us, though later, my sister-in-law and a cousin joined us. The silence was solid, broken only by the monotonous, repetitive and rasping song of the cicadas that inhabited the coniferous trees surrounding the cemetery. To that music, the two men began their digging, shovelling steadily at my mother's grave. We stood silently, watching as the dry, dusty earth was dug up and piled at the side of the grave; it took a very long time to find any trace of human remains. The men sweated, stopped and started, then spoke in Albanian. One started to pull with both hands and brought up a skull; my mother's head was now a bony sculpture. The digger held it up to me and I received it tearfully, tenderly, as though it were a newly delivered baby.

My mother's head. Her lovely wavy hair, the soft skin on her cheeks, her green eyes and beautiful mouth all vanished, all gone forever, devoured by the earth. My tears fell silently and profusely waiting by the graveside for more parts of what once was our mother. Picked up by one or the other digger, the smaller fragments of bone were difficult to identify. I collected them carefully. A small hair comb—how poignant. My mother must have put it in her hair the day she died. A bit of plastic had survived. But when the pelvic bones were handed to me, another wave of sorrow overwhelmed me, and I could hardly speak. My voice was tremulous as I tried to tell my brothers that all five of us had passed through this very passage out of her body. What great pain she must have endured in childbirth, and with no pain relief whatsoever.

All of our mother's bones that the earth had not swallowed up were gradually retrieved and handed to me, all crumbling at the edges. Those were the arms that had held me, her first-born, for the first time and cradled me as she had with the other four children after me. The hands that fed us, washed us, clothed us; the hands that steadied us when we took our first steps and guided us.

We, the three women, washed the bones in water and in wine, and laid them on a white cloth to dry in the sun. My father had been dead only for thirteen years, so the diggers soon reached the level of his remains. When they did, my tears began to flow down my face again. No one spoke at all, except the diggers in their native tongue.

Father died at the age of 75, eighteen years after our mother. In his case, I was there at his funeral and in time to keep the overnight vigil with the rest of the family. He lay in his open coffin covered in his favourite flower—red camellias—with only his head and face visible. He looked, I remembered, as if he were sleeping, and so much younger a man, with a full head of dark hair, well into his 70s. Now, by the graveside, I was handed another skull, and I felt once again the same feelings as I experienced when my mother's skull was pressed into my hands. Our tall, strong, handsome father towered over most people in the village. Iraclis was his name, and like the Hercules of Greek mythology, he too was a giant. The evidence of his structure lay in the width and weight of his bones. I remember his hands were as big as dinner plates. But where was that giant now? The graves had robbed us, had swallowed up the whole man and given us back only his bones and his watch.

We washed his bones in water and wine and laid them out on the white cloth next to our mother, to dry in the sun. Our parents, or what was left of them, lay side by side, resting together in the sun and waiting for their family to gather them up and find yet another resting-place. We put both parents' remains in one, specially commissioned wooden box. We included two photographs of them in their youth, then covered them with a white lacy cloth and closed the box. It was heavy. We took it into the ossuary and placed it beside our mother's sister, Aunt Kitsa.

I plan to visit the village at Easter 2008 and will, of course, go to the cemetery again. I wonder what it will hold for me this time, or the next time. Will the eucalyptus tree beckon me? Will I want to open the casket? Will I dissolve into tears, or have I mourned enough? It will never be enough, I know. For as long as I live, I will continue to mourn her and to ask her departed soul to forgive me.

We departed from the cemetery in silence that day, many hours later. The sun was descending in the sky: His fire was already directed elsewhere.

DESTINATION: THESSALONIKI

March is by far the most turbulent and unpredictable month of the year. The wind is heavily charged with a fierce chill factor that defies the warmth of the sun to offer comfort. It is so cold it has been known to force people to pull up their hedges from the Grecian earth, to gather anything at all that will produce a flame in the hearth for a while. They even burn the furniture, just to survive its icy wrath.

The sea doesn't escape the spring moodiness, but it is lulled, now and again, long enough to convince the unwary that it will be safe and calm for a trip across the ocean.

Heavily pregnant, my young mother embarked on a voyage aboard a motorboat, to go and be delivered of her first baby in the safety of a hospital. Our village, close to the cold slopes of Mount Athos, lacked any medical services: no nursing at all, not even midwifery. So, on March 24th, her odyssey to Thessaloniki began.

It began on a beautiful day. The sun made the sea placid and gloriously calm. Its wide expanse from Ouranoupolis (the first finger of Halkidiki, across to Sithonia), sparkled as if seeded with crystals. Cutting a watery furrow through the sea, they rode the path of the sea-horses, headed in a south-easterly direction to set them on the right course.

Halfway across, nearing the Cape of Sithonia, the sea suddenly rose up like a mountain; the waves threatened to engulf the tiny vessel as it rocked and tossed about like flotsam. Panic-stricken passengers believed the end was nigh. The pitching sea below and the raging storm without induced in my mother a premature labour.

Even the safe haven within my mother's womb failed to prevent my distress; her labour intensified and no one could do anything at all to help her. How much she must have feared the outcome, out there on the ocean, giving birth in a boat! Might it not have been safer to have remained in our primitive village after all? But, as fate would have it, I held on fast, despite the rough waters hurling me sideways and willy-nilly, furiously up and down.

Eventually, after our perilous voyage, we reached the relative safety of the harbour. I was ready to emerge from my watery cell even as my mother was carried off into a nearby house and laid down on a bed to rest. The storm was over. We were on firm, dry land—a much better stage for making my entrance. So, out I slipped, and by all accounts, I yelled the house down! A tiny scrap of humanity, no bigger, our mother would often recount, than our kitchen scissors, but with such a giant of a voice. A tiny babe with a fury to level mountains, I was.

Life for me, from birth to age fourteen, was a normal enough childhood for one raised in a poor village in northern Greece...at least, normal enough. But from the age of ten to fourteen, I had to grow up fast and participate in most domestic and outdoor tasks, not least of which was the care of my new baby brother. His arrival signalled such a rapid decline in our mother's already fragile health due to chronic bronchial asthma that my workload increased until I fancied I was almost a little mother myself.

I remember now, with regret and great shame, how I one time threatened suicide by drowning. I actually ran to the sea, walked to the water's edge, and deposited my tiny wooden clogs there, to make it look as though I had already entered my anticipated grave. I then walked back on myself and crouched by the hedge of shrubs, waiting for someone to find me.

My mother arrived and there was no sign of me except for my footwear at the water's edge. As selfish as I was, I couldn't stand her despairing of my presumed fate. I had to give myself up to calm and comfort her. After all these long years, I can't remember what was said, but there was no anger in her for my trickery: the relief of finding me alive made words unnecessary.

My life, I now suspect, is a reflection of that tempestuous voyage by sea that gave birth to me.

OURANOUPOLIS

At the dawn of my existence, when I first became aware of my surroundings and other individuals, I believed that my maternal grandmother, who lived with us, had given birth to all the people in the universe, the cosmos, our little village. I had no idea that there were other villages or human beings elsewhere in the great wide world.

Our village, Ouranoupolis, was new in comparison to the ancient country surrounding us. It was built on land that belonged to the Republic of Athos: a mountainous peninsula that starts from the borders of the village of Nea Rhoda near the Xerxes' Canal in Tripiti, where it is about two kilometres wide. As it progresses eastwards, it expands sideways until eventually it appears as though it rises out of the sea. It is studded with monasteries; most of them perched on the cliffs that fall precipitously to the deep blue sea below. The mountain, Athos itself, increases in height until it reaches over two thousand metres—its peak often seen with an icing of snow; although, at other times, it can also be shrouded in mist. Athos dominates everything, descending majestically to meet the angry Aegean and plunging to its pitiless and fathomless depths. Here lies the watery tomb of the invading Persian army of Xerxes. Two helmets, encrusted with sea fossils and alleged to be relics of the infamous disaster, are now exhibited in the Tower museum.

Mount Athos, often referred to as the Holy Mountain, is out of bounds to women. This is due to Mary, the Panagia (all holy one), mother of Jesus Christ, allegedly having landed there in a storm and claiming it as her garden. No female of any species is permitted to set foot on it, as it is the sole domain of the Mother. During the summer, visitors from our village and from Sithonia, in the middle finger of Halkidiki, view the Athos peninsula from cruise ships, which, because they have women on board, are only permitted to sail within five hundred metres of the shore. Part of this holy mountain was commandeered by the Greek government on behalf of the Greek exiles returning from the Princes' Isles near Istanbul in Asia Minor and from Caesarea.

Ouranoupolis is about two kilometres from the Athos border. The road leading there threads itself along uneven terrain, dusty in the summer and muddy in the winter. At times, it glimpses the sea; at the next turn, it passes through wooded country. At one time, there were no houses between the village and Arsanas, the monastery on the border. Since the sixties, however, both sides of the road have been filled with hotels and self-catering accommodation for the tourists.

Before tourism came, there was no physical barrier between Arsanas and the village. We, the children, freely ventured onto the monastic land. In fact, we often went along with the adults, carrying a basket with eggs for the monks. As no female animals were allowed to live and reproduce in the Virgin's garden, eggs and milk were most welcome at the monastery. The entrance to this monastery was guarded by a heavy door. We would call out, "Father Shepherd!" in our shrill, childish voices and continue to yell until we were heard.

The loud thud of the monk's boots on the stone yard announced his arrival. He took a long time—so it seemed to us—to unlock the door, turn the key, remove the chains, draw the bolts and lift the latch. He looked old and tall in his black robes: his black pillbox hat, his hair in a knot resting on the nape of his neck, and his greying beard reaching down almost to his waist. I believe he was glad to see us, although he never said as much. But then, I do not recollect a conversation of any substance, anyway. His eyes went straight to the basket and its contents. He always looked pleased in his own monkish way. We would hand it over and watch both him and the basket disappear behind the fortress door.

Time goes so slowly for the young; we would wriggle and fidget while he was gone, impatiently but quietly awaiting his return. His heavy footsteps would eventually come nearer, the bolt and chains removed, and a benevolent monk would appear with our basket for us, full of fresh vegetables like tomatoes, aubergines,

17

beetroot, onions and marrows. Oh, what joy it was for us!

The monastery had plenty of fresh water, hence the abundance of the earth's gifts to the monks. We in the village, on the other hand, had precious little of it. We had to draw it from wells dug deep in the earth, and people often became very ill after drinking it. One young woman was so ill, in fact, that all her hair fell out. Subsequently, I learnt that this was the result of typhoid fever. The offending well was in her family garden—an area used as an outdoor cinema. We used to sit on makeshift benches there, but not for long—for rats would scurry under our feet. We fled—terrified—screaming in alarm and forgetting the film, which was silent anyway. I believe, on reflection, that rats or lice were the most likely cause of that particular episode of typhoid fever.

The site for our village was first known as Prosphorion (A Gift), then changed to Pyrgos (Tower), and finally to its present title of Ouranoupolis (Sky City). It was chosen by the League of Nations without due consideration for its new inhabitants, the refugees of the war. There was no water, sanitation, or electricity. Nor were there any means of communication with other fellow humans and no transport. The nearest habitation was seven kilometres away in Nea Rhoda. It could only be reached on foot or by mule (if one possessed such an animal), by donkey (if one were available), and in summer, by rowing a boat to Tripiti then continuing on foot to Nea Rhoda to consult with Dr. Marinos for treatment of the various ailments so frequent among the people.

The houses where we lived were imitation bungalows—empty—lacking even the basic necessities for a simple existence. For my grandparents, once comfortable and affluent in Asia Minor, it must have been extremely hard indeed to adjust to such nakedly primitive conditions. All their property and most of their goods had been left behind, and most of what they had brought with them had been sold simply to stay alive in their new home.

As the village was constructed on land that had, for one thousand years, belonged to Mount Athos, and which the Mother of Jesus the Panagia called her own, it was not surprising that the earth here was hostile, the soil arid and barren, refusing to be fruitful, and reducing the new inhabitants to abject poverty. Water, the essential element for existence was scarcely adequate for human

18

life; very little could be spared for agriculture.

The dwellings were in rows along the seafront on the south and in the same neat rows on the west, again along the seafront. Both rows began from the famous Tower, built by Andronicus Paleologos the Second. The Tower, where the helmets from the sea are now displayed, is a landmark visible from a great distance—a welcoming sight for the traveller these days. Providing beautiful weather and all the facilities for a luxurious holiday, the modern village has become a very popular tourist resort. The village creeps up on sloping ground to a hilly countryside. From that level of the hills, the view is of olive trees descending all the way to the fringes of the houses, so that the entire village appears as a tiny triangle, the Tower at its point. That monument always looks as if it arises out from the ocean, standing tall and dominant, looking down silently over upwards of one hundred Lilliputian buildings.

And in that little village was my home.

Our Home

Our house was identical to all the village homes; it differed only in its use of the interior. There were two large and one tiny bedroom, an entrance hall and a kitchen. The kitchen served as a multifunctional room in purpose: a dining room, bathroom, family room, a bedroom, and a treatment-room. In the winter, heat was generated from the fireplace in the kitchen, which took up an entire corner in an already confined space, but was nevertheless a most appreciated commodity. It provided a means, however inadequate, for heating and cooking.

A further source for improving the room temperature was the mangali or brazier, a circular copper or tin container. It was about thirty centimetres in circumference and ten centimetres in depth, supported on four sturdy metal legs. The base had a thick layer of ashes, and when a shovelful of hot coals from the kitchen fire was emptied on this soft bed, the effect was remarkable: the heat dissipated fast about the room. I remember Cousin Marina leaping from the settee one time as children, catching her sock on the handle of the mangali and tipping it over on the floor. Fortunately, the coals had lost their first heat. They had blackened and failed to burn the floor rug.

But the mangali was popular with us for popcorn. When the coals were no longer fierce, a flour sieve with a measure of popcorn, covered with a tea towel to stop the popping corn from escaping, was held over it. This task had to be undertaken by an adult because the sieve had to be held firmly, and at the same time, tossed from side to side in order to give the corn a uniform exposure for a successful flowering, which would fill the sieve and bulge under the tea towel. The snow-white popped corn looked like little flowers edged with gold. It was emptied on to a metal tray, sprinkled with salt, and placed on the floor. We swooped down on it like greedy sea gulls and devoured it at similar speed.

The kitchen ceiling was incomplete: It ended short of one metre. This space between the roof and the ceiling was used as a shelf to store footwear. I often dreamed of finding a pair of red shoes there for myself, though this was only a dream. Grandma would tell me that it was simply "the hungry dream of bread."

My sisters and I discovered a toothbrush on that shelf; it must have been very old. The handle looked like a piece of yellow bone, its bristles stiff and off white. We made use of it in turn, dipping it in cooking salt and brushing our teeth vigorously. It made our gums sore, so we abandoned it. Our dental routine was neglected thereafter. I would not have believed in the huge variety of toothbrushes, including battery-operated brushes, available to me in later life and to my children and grandchildren early in theirs.

The back entrance to our home was from the garden through the kitchen, which was on the south side of the house. To the right of the door was the sink, with two shelves beneath it for the cooking utensils, and above it was a container for the water with a tap fixed to the wall. We replenished that water every day, fetching it, of course, from the well. There was no luxury of running water at that time. Next to the sink was a small window and below it a stool: a popular place to sit, as it was next to the hearth.

Along the east side stretched a settee underneath another window, our lookout for potential quarry. It was from that very spot we plotted, planned and trapped unwary birds as snacks to supplement our poor diet. Next to the window from where we watched the birds, beside the chimney breast, stood our larder in the shape of a rectangular cage. It was covered on three sides with a fine wire mesh and two shelves for food. Our parents chose to place it high up to prevent us children from raiding it!

A single bed/settee took up most of the north wall, allowing space for just a couple of chairs. There was a paraffin lamp hung on a nail above it with a glass reservoir and a wick that looked like a flattened-out, pickled worm. A pear-shaped glass cover sat on the reservoir on a circular base through which the wick emerged. Our mother lit the lamp when the natural light faded with the departure of the sun. As the evening became night and we went to bed, she lowered the wick; the light diminished and extinguished. By this time, the glass mantle became so blackened it would need a thorough clean. Mamma would undertake this task the following day when the delicate glass would have cooled.

Along the west wall of the kitchen, a table and two chairs led to the little room that completed the kitchen furnishings—a little room that was in fact a bedroom. A wall-to-wall bed took up most of the space. Four of us shared this small platform. Poor Grandma slept with us and had to keep the peace between all three siblings. We possessed no teddy bears or other cuddly toys to hold and be comforted by as we recounted any frightening events that were occupying our young minds.

Sleeping four in a bed, we were hot in the summer, but not so in the winter when shared body heat was a welcome comfort. We warmed ourselves with smooth stones from the beach and heated them in the hot embers of the kitchen fire. We took care to avoid contact burns by sprinkling them with water, which produced a warm steam. When it evaporated, we wrapped them in old clothing and placed them at the foot of the bed. It was a far cry from the rubber hot water bottles in fleecy covers or electric blankets that I enjoyed later in life.

Out from this bedroom, we stepped into the hall. Along the wall, on the left side, was a cupboard with a display cabinet on top. It contained some pretty china, a few primary school books, and a Greek-English dictionary belonging to our father. As we didn't know the Latin alphabet, it was of little benefit to us. We also had three children's books in English. They were given to us by the Menzies girls, (their father Colonel Menzies was in charge of the Canadian War Graves Commission) Jill and Hazel, who spent summer holidays in our village with their parents and governess. We loved looking at the books; it was the first time we had seen colourful illustrations. We pretended to read the writing, making up our own stories. Two books were about Rupert Bear. He looked so bright and happy in his yellow checked trousers and red coat. The third book was big and heavy; it was in black and white and had hard paper pages. It displayed Mickey Mouse and friends, shown within a fence, which was held upright by a large snake entwined between the wooden stakes. We made up dramatic stories out of the pictures, as we had come across real snakes and were terrified by them.

The display cabinet extended to the end of the south wall, which led to the west, to a door opening into the master bedroom—a place of family joys, sorrows, suffering, and mourning. Too often mourning. This unfortunate room had one wardrobe on the left, with a bed beside it and two windows—one facing the sunset, a settee below it with many small cushions, all embroidered by grandma in colourful silks. Above that settee hung the only picture in the entire house—a picture that had survived the exile from Turkey. It depicted an exceptionally strong man, who, I now think, must have been Hercules executing one of his Labours: his arms were round the neck of a ferocious lion. This bright artwork was from grandma's dowry; she had done all the intricate work herself, with tiny beads in various colours sewn on black velvet. To this day, even after the upgrading of the property, it still occupies more or less the same position.

The chamber's second window was on the north side, under which lay an ottoman full of bedding, taking up more or less all of the space. Next to it sat a triangular dressing table, fitted snugly between the north and east sides. I remember very clearly a mirror, hairbrushes, a comb, a round box with powder and hairpins, with many more items occupying the lower shelves.

The bare wooden floor resembled a drawing board: it was crisscrossed with lines—some horizontal, others oblique and curved. There were triangles and circles, too, all made by our father when he was busy designing his first boat.

Coming out of this room and turning left, there in the corner under the window stood a giant earthenware storage container with a lid like a tabletop. In this, we kept the olive oil, out of light and beyond the reach of mice. The flat lid provided Grandma with a good place for the covered bowl of primed milk to turn into yogurt. Beside the container was the front door of the house, opening to the wide outside world and all its daily events.

There was, however, another bedroom opposite the master bedroom, across the hall. It was a big bedroom, cold even though it faced the morning sun. Its ceiling was only partly complete. I remember looking up from where I lay on the floor, sobbing with long ago earache, seeing the exposed red roof tiles. There was one window facing north that was seldom open, and under it laid a rectangular wooden storage container on legs for the flour. After the harvest each year, we would take the wheat to the miller, and in due course, fetch it back again as flour. Leaving it in sacks would have amounted to an invitation to the mice to have their own harvest. On one such occasion, I watched as both my parents were engaged in transferring the flour from the sacks into the container, and my father made deep indentations in the flour with a wooden pole. I was curious and asked the reason for this. He said they were traps for the mice to fall into. What a joke to play on a small child! However, Mamma explained to me he was compressing the flour to increase the storage capacity, so that more flour could be added.

Next to the east window stood a single bed. It was there, in that bed that, on the 7th of February, 1937, the other of our two brothers was born. His birth had elements of a great surprise for me, but that is for another time.

Stepping out in to the hall, we find two low wooden armchairs, crafted by our kind, paternal grandfather, known to everybody in the village as Barba Yiannis. Apart from sitting to watch the world go by, this little square space was also used to store the olives until they were taken to the olive press.

Our kitchen also served as a bedroom and a bathroom. Our father had constructed wooden rectangular troughs, each dedicated according to its purpose: one was for bread making, another was for laundry, and the third was for bathing and hair washing. Another use of the kitchen—though only in the winter—was as a place to offer the advice and remedies provided by our mother to the many village people who presented with a variety of ailments. In the summer, such therapies were performed in the garden, in the cool shade of the vine.

The toilet was at the top of the garden, where our father made for us a luxury lavatory. In common with all the other houses in the village, our home had no proper toilet. During the cold winter months, we made use of chamber pots kept under the beds. In summer, we were able to use our special outdoor toilet, which was entirely unique. No squatting over a hole in the ground for our family! Our father built a three-sided thatched dwelling, roughly the size of a telephone kiosk. On the roof, he fixed a weather vane made from a bicycle wheel. He made a rectangular seat, like a bench with a panelled front. I remember sitting on it and dangling my feet against it, too small to reach the floor. He cut a circular opening, small enough to prevent us from falling through, yet adequate for adult comfort too. This he placed securely over a pit. Our mother made a curtain out of brown sacking to provide privacy, and we were very proud indeed of our toilet. We'd boast about its safety and comfort to our friends, as children are want to do.

One incident happened, however, while I was using the super-loo. I heard footsteps and glimpsed through the side of the curtain. I saw my father approaching but became paralysed with fear, quite unable to speak or warn him I was there. I waited; he came up and relieved himself against the thatched side of the building. He was quite unaware of my presence, but in my haste to make myself invisible to him, I rushed out and found myself directly in front of him. He was furious. He shouted at me and at Mamma. I was crying and insisting that I had not seen any naked part of him at all, but to no avail: He just glared at me instead.

The family home was, in the end, left to Angeliki, our sister. It was upgraded—only the outer shell was left intact - but the interior was transformed into a luxurious dwelling with all the modern facilities. It has a fireplace now, which heats the lounge on chilly evenings; no longer does it belch out black smoke. The central heating is fired by petrogaz in large drums. In the hot weather, air conditioning provides cool breezes throughout.

No more washing up with bran as a detergent. No more rinsing the dishes under a slow tap that had to be filled with water from the village well. Now there is a dishwasher, and laundry, too, is done by machine. There is an electric cooker with an oven—how Grandma would have appreciated the facility, as she did most of the cooking when our mother was ill. I remember her saying how much easier life would be if only food would come in pill form like medicines. Had she managed to live longer than her ninety-two years, she would have seen her wish come true in the diet we serve to the astronauts in space.

MOTHER

Our mother was born in Asia Minor in 1909. She was named Vassiliki. She was the youngest of three daughters. She was a pretty child with light brown hair and green eyes. But it was her happy disposition and sunny nature that made her popular with all who had contact with the family; her parents adored her. Moreover, from a very early age, our mother (whom I shall now refer to as Mamma, a name by which mothers are addressed in my old country), showed very distinct signs of enterprise and initiative.

Even as a nine-year-old, during the family's first exile in Asia Minor, she observed when in the marketplace the large consumption of bread rolls bought by the businessmen for their mid-morning break. Before their exile, the family had owned a bakery; the child knew a little about the output and variety of bread that they had produced. She suggested to her father that he set up at once as a bread-roll merchant.

"We cannot afford to buy the flour, my child," she was told. But her solution to this problem was already solved: "We can use maize flour and sell the rolls hot, straight out of the oven, before they get hard, can't we, Father?"

In due course, the rolls were baked, and young Vassiliki, along with an older sister, made innumerable journeys carrying panniers lined with white linen tablecloths, within whose folds were nestled warm maize rolls for the marketplace, where the hungry Turks devoured them with relish. So it was that, through a child's observation, enough money was earned to buy wheat flour and, during that first exile, start the bakery business once more. Regrettably, despite my mother's ingenuity, the business was lost to them again when they were exiled for a second time.

26

That clever child, who briefly lifted her family out poverty and despair, eventually became our mother, 'Mamma,' as we addressed her then, and still do whenever we mention her.

As an adult, Mamma suffered from chronic bronchial asthma, a debilitating condition. Breathing became increasingly difficult and laborious: coughing was constant, very distressing and exhausting, bringing up horrible thick phlegm, which I remember made me feel distinctly sick as it was spat out into a pot. Little did I know back then, of course, that in the future, in my chosen career as a nurse, I would have to empty many a potful of spit out of enamel containers, which held the cloying contents firmly in their interior. That was back in the age of non-disposable containers and the absence of gloves, so once more I was to feel sick, and yes, I gagged.

During her asthma attacks, Mamma could only sleep in the sitting position, though even then her coughing and breathing were just as troublesome, waking her up gasping for breath, becoming blue in her face. For us as young children, it was deeply frightening; we feared for her life in case the breathing stopped altogether. We were terrified she would choke. We would go to her but could not help her. It probably distressed her more to see our anxiety and her complete inability to reassure us. We were sympathetic and always eager to offer help, but I am ashamed to admit that we resented her illness. It stopped us joining other children's fun. But that was very selfish of us, and I still feel guilty about it, even now.

The first asthma attack our mother had to suffer was apparently at the age of seven. The problem seemed to disappear by the time she reached puberty, but then returned with a vengeance during her second pregnancy. The size of her abdomen had warned of a multiple birth, and twins were delivered in due course. In November 1932, Mamma went into labour; she was taken to a hospital erected under canvas, a temporary hospital set up to treat the victims of a recent earthquake; their village Ierissos, had been totally destroyed only two months earlier.

Worse than that, it was a journey of about twenty kilometres, which must have been agony for the patient in strong labour, being transported by ox cart with no available pain relief. The hospital provided medical professionals through the Red Cross, who

27

successfully delivered my mother's twin girls. But the patient's condition was extremely poor due to excessive blood loss, and transfusions were not an option. The patient felt unbearably cold. It was a very severe winter with a heavy snowfall in a hospital hopelessly exposed to the elements. Mamma felt so weak she was convinced that she would die.

Our Grandmother told us that Mamma would never fully recover after giving birth to the twins and then breastfeeding them for many months thereafter. No mother, of course, had any choice about that, as breastfeeding was simply the cheapest, most convenient and the best food for the babies. It was not, however, good for a mother in such a weakened condition. Her asthma thus returned in continuous and aggressive attacks for the rest of her life. Two more pregnancies at four yearly intervals caused further deterioration of her already fragile health.

Once again, another baby was on the way. There were three girls, already: one under five, and the twins, who were both under four. It was then that I most remember the hardship of her life. How very difficult it was for Mamma and our Grandma, even when well, to care for us, to care in a household that had no heating, no running water, no electricity, and having to rely on oil lamps and a toilet away from the house at the top of garden.

No wonder that I cannot remember any quality time spent with our mother. I cannot recollect being hugged, cuddled or read to by her, though she did teach me how to read by myself, and not in syllables, like most.

"Look at the next word quickly, then you will half-recognise it before you have to pronounce it," she would say, and it did work— no help was required from an adult reading my schoolbooks for me. Of course, we only had a few books anyway, none for children except the ones from the Menzies girls, which were in English, a foreign tongue to me at that time.

It was Mamma, too, who taught me my very first song. It took a very long time to memorise the words and to learn to sing in tune. She also taught me the rudiments of embroidery. She herself produced fine lacework, with no more than an ordinary sewing needle, and intricate designs with a crochet hook. I still have a few

28

items of her work and treasure them with pride and admiration.

Grandma would have been too busy from sunrise to sunset, caring for the family, to have the time for telling stories to her grandchildren. Yet she made time to teach me how to spin lamb's wool and goat hair, milk the goats, and how to make yogurt and cheese, for I followed her around as she performed all these tasks and more. Eventually, I did spin enough wool myself to dye it green and knit myself a dress. I was thirteen years old and very proud of my achievement. Disaster struck when I washed the garment, however; it went out of shape to such an extent that it could never be worn again.

Spinning the coarse goat hair was tough on the fingers, but it made strong rope, a very useful commodity for tethering the animals and attaching to buckets for drawing water from wells. From my Grandmother, then, I learned to be useful.

Useful or not, it was sons, not a daughter, that my father wanted. It was to be sons. Like many men, even now when we know that it is the father's genes that predetermine the sex of the baby, he felt that his manhood was under threat. He was very angry with our mother; he was furious with her for presenting him with three little girls in three years. He was entirely determined to bring forth sons despite his wife's perilously fragile health, the lack of space in our little home and our continued dependence on Grandmother.

As I was the first child, my father had gradually come to terms with the disaster, looking with hope to the future no doubt. Indeed, he built a snowman to welcome me, a giant by all accounts. Although my father was two metres tall, he had to stand on a ladder to add the head and make the face. The snow sculpture dominated the village square and was there for a while, to celebrate my arrival, although at once my father promptly deserted home for a full six months, leaving his wife and baby daughter to be cared for by his in-laws. He betrayed us and deserted us. And this was not a single isolated incident; it happened again after the birth of the twin girls, and many, many more times thereafter, until in his fifties, he finally took himself off for good. Our Mamma, ill as she was, was abandoned by him, even as her health grew worse.

29

March 24: Today is my birthday. Mamma became pregnant before her marriage; her parents must have been very enlightened indeed, for this was the 1930s, to offer as they did to bring up the baby, so that my mother was not obliged to marry the father. As it happened, the young ones were entirely in love—a transitory love, as things turned out. But I was born to a married couple.

Eighteen months later, when my twin sisters were born, he was desperately angry and extremely upset, disappointed, inconsolable. Mamma's sister told him it served him right for having been so unkind, insensitive, and thoughtless, distressing our mother when I was born a girl and making her so unhappy. But his rage persisted.

There is an image of a child locked in my memory, a little girl crouching for safety beneath a pregnant abdomen. That terrified individual is me, and I still remember the event vividly, even though it was so long ago that it seems now as if I was no more than an observer of my past self.

Mamma was standing in the kitchen, our multi-functional room. I cannot recollect how I arrived there and hid between her legs, but I could see my father's giant legs firmly planted astride, like the Colossus of Rhodes, directly in front of me. Worse, I could hear the swish of his whip, and even glimpsed it as he was slicing the air with it. Why was he so angry with me? Or perhaps, was it our mother he was trying to punish? She kept imploring and pleading with him to stop: "In the name of God, stop!"

I have no real explanation for such violence, because I cannot remember why it began or how it ended, nor can I say which one of our brothers was in the comparative safety of our mother's womb. I wonder to this day what psychological distress, or even permanent damage, the personality of that foetus might have undergone that day.

Our father was very tall and broad. He stood like a great tree. We feared him, and so did his sons and grandsons. He proved to be liberal with the cane and his heavy fists. He did, nonetheless, have good qualities as well, but those are for a different discourse.

Our mother, whenever freed from her asthma, was remarkably swift in turning her attention to all domestic duties. Enthusiastic, thrifty, imaginative, she was an enterprising cook who could provide a meal out of whatever common ingredients were at hand, in the garden, in the sea or in the countryside. Our father would send a message to Mamma, telling her that another friend would be joining the family for lunch one day. Seldom did he provide the goods or the money; but somehow, Mamma always could get a meal together.

Some of her recipes stick with me still: Wild Boar Meat Preserves, for example. On the odd occasions when my father and his friends managed to shoot a wild boar, it a was time for celebration in the family, though even then it was a lot of hard work for our mother, as she was the one who would have to preserve as much of our share as she possibly could. Meat was a rare luxury in our household, so it was always necessary to make provision for lean times that frequently visited us.

Our mother minced the pork in the old heavy hand-mincer, then seasoned it with herbs, kneaded it, and stuffed it into tubes made out of strips cut from cotton cloth that had been sewn by her on the treadle sewing machine. She patted the bulging tubes with her hands to flatten them, then measured each section with her palm to ensure that all were the same size, then tying each portion with a short piece of string. Each tube was suspended on a hook inside the fireplace to slowly cure in the eye-smarting smoke, which was forever belching down the chimney into the kitchen.

A section of smoked wild boar-meat cooked with chickpeas, haricot or broad beans, was truly a feast. Our staple diet, I am afraid, was very dull: lentils, chickpeas, haricot beans, dried broad beans. We also ate the latter uncooked instead of biscuits, because we simply hadn't any. Many years later, an English friend told me that during that same war, she and her siblings had been evacuated to Wales, where they made quite a habit of stealing broken biscuits from the pigs' trough. I found it hard to believe—is there no justice in the world? What sort of farmer in Wales could afford to buy biscuits meant for human consumption, broken or not, and feed them to his pigs, in times of war? There were no such men in my village.

In Greece, men often hunted to try and feed their families. My father had been known to shoot an occasional hare, which made

31

the most satisfying meal: stifatho—what is known here as 'jugged hare.' Mamma was an expert at making that meal, which our father would announce was "fit for a king!"

Her nursing skills were even more valued. Mamma was a deeply compassionate woman. Her own illness made her much more understanding of others in need of healing and help. Whenever she was free from asthma, she attended to anyone who sought her assistance. Some of her remedies and treatment may well appear outdated and unscientific when considered today, but her empathy and her practical application invariably made people feel better.

On so many occasions, I watched Mamma perform her remedies, heal and help, and I often watched her work as a horticulturalist too. All her energies seemed to be given to the cultivation of life.

Our mother, for example, grafted wild pear trees and vines, with cuttings given by male grafting enthusiasts. They admired and encouraged her for having the courage to join in an activity normally undertaken only by men. I was fascinated by her technique and was eager to watch and learn, though before I left home at fourteen, I didn't have a chance to experiment.

Mamma would select a young branch of wild pear and pull it gently to eye level. With a sharp knife, she would cut a horizontal line on the bark, about six centimetres long and eight centimetres across, making a cross. Using the point of the knife, she would part and lift the bark, exposing the naked area to receive the graft. Picking up the tender cutting bearing two buds or little eyes, she would trim it to a slither, moisten it with saliva in her mouth and insert it in the gaping slit of the cross. Mamma then brought the bark edges together, partly imprisoning the little intruder. The graft was firmly secured to the parent branch with a bandage of raffia and left to grow in the embrace of its surrogate mother: the 'little eyes' would be following the sun on its celestial journey to the end of the day and winking at the twinkling stars in the darkness of the night. We hoped that eventually the graft would take over the character of its host, and produce edible fruit.

When Mamma was less troubled by her asthma and well

enough for a walk in the countryside, she and I would wander up to inspect the grafts. I followed because I was eager to see new life emerging from the buds as they unfolded, and watching tiny green leaves appear filled me with excitement. On the occasions when the graft remained inert, blind and wooden, Mamma and I shared a great disappointment.

Grafting on vines required a different approach. Mamma had to use one of our father's saws to cut through the stringy and tough outer covering of the selected branch. The amputated limb was allowed to fall unceremoniously to the earth below. The exposed flat surface was criss-crossed across its circumference to a depth of about five centimetres. Where the two lines crossed, they were parted with the point of the knife to make space for the uninvited guest. Its host accepted it: it had no choice but to nurture it.

As with the pear graft, the preparation was the same. Following the graft implantation, the receiving branch was firmly bandaged with raffia and a wet mixture of soil and straw was placed on the surface, looking like a miniature dome with part of the graft bearing the buds or 'little eyes' poking through like a chimney. This dome would preserve the rising sap from being lost through evaporation and provide sustenance for the growth of the graft.

Sometimes these grafts worked, sometimes they didn't. When new growth emerged, it filled me always with immense excitement, as so often and in so many ways, Mamma had succeeded in encouraging life.

Our Father

Our father was born in Asia Minor, in a small village quite different from the one in which Mamma was brought into the world. He was the eldest of four siblings, a sister and two boys, both of whom died during the second exile, en route to the Turkish interior. My father survived, as he survived much else. Our parents met in Greece in 1926, in the Peloponese where the authorities placed them in a private, three-bedroom house shared with two other exiled families. The domestic facilities were poor and inadequate, but worse was to follow—much worse—when they were finally brought to our present village of Ouranoupolis in 1928

My father's mother was very short: barely four-feet tall. In no time at all her son overtook her, and consequently, she looked up to her darling son quite literally; in fact, she worshipped him. No young woman was good enough for him, and when it was disclosed that the future bride was older than the groom (albeit by one year!), Grandma was incensed: she nearly had apoplexy!

Neither Grandma nor her daughter, my Aunt Olga, liked our mother. They always resented her and caused many problems for the young couple. Grandfather Yiannis, on the other hand, was always kind, supportive and generous, offering gifts of fish and fruit or making wooden clogs for us. Making things, as it turned out, ran in the family: like father like son.

Our father's name was Iraclis (Hercules) and like his namesake, he was powerfully built and strong. He evoked fear more than affection in the household. He was feared by all, both the immediate and eventually extended family, who were unfortunate enough to live together or in close proximity. He was over two metres tall; his head was generously endowed with dark brown hair, which remained abundant well into his old age. His eyes were almost black, his eyebrows also black and well defined. Sometimes he sported an auburn moustache, the same colour as my hair in my youth. His teeth were even and sound and he retained them to the end of his life.

His limbs were long and thick. His hands were big and strong. He could break a brick in two with those bare hands, and I saw him do the same with a plank of wood. He strode with ease, upright and with an air of authority, and was very handsome. He played the mandolin with pathos and sang too, melodiously and harmoniously. He would have liked to have been an actor and, as I discovered from his youthful photographs, he possessed the looks of one as well.

He was very clever at inventing and constructing. He was always ingenious. He designed his first model boat on the floor of the front (and best) room of our home, making the wooden floor his drawing board, as he had no paper. One year, when Easter was fast approaching, our parents collaborated to make three pairs of sandals for us, their little girls. Father measured our feet by standing each one of us on the wood destined to become the sandal platforms, and then drawing the shape of our feet upon it with the pencil he kept behind his ear: that was his trademark, that of the carpenter and furniture maker.

He cut out the shape of the foot, and then cut again at the point where the toes begin from the main body of the foot. This was to provide a flexible joint. He nailed a thin strip of leather and joined the two parts, enabling us to walk more freely by bending the toe part of the sole. In the meantime, Mamma cut strips of white sailcloth and blue strips from an old dress. This she sewed over the white base and made four of these for each sandal —twenty-four in all. Two strips were needed to cross over the front of the foot, one to go round the ankle and the front across it, to secure the sandal. The buckles were recycled from worn-out footwear.

It was springtime. The almond and peach trees were covered in blossoms. They looked like giant brides. It was, in fact, Easter day itself when three little girls stepped out in new sandals and dressed in frocks that looked just as new, even though they were made from recycled material, as well, thanks to our mother's dexterity. Our parents must have been justly pleased and proud to see us walk to church for the Easter celebration service on that sunny morning. It was such a long time ago—a memory to be relived and cherished. There are so many of those memories…

"I have good news for you," our father announced one morning. "We will not need that open fire anymore." He was immensely confident, thoroughly persuaded that the brand-new construction he had in mind would provide us with all the heat and cooking energy we required. That stove in our kitchen, plus the fireplace in the corner with the chimney that was guaranteed to belch out smoke, even if there was no more than a whiff of wind outside, were unbearable for us at times. We in turn became very excited, impatient to know just when he was going to start, and if it would be ready for the cold winter weather.

"Yes, it will be," he assured us. "We must start right now, to get the mud bricks ready to sun-bake." He suggested that we help.

This was heavy work for men. As for children, however, we merely made a game of it, offering to assist by fetching water and straw. Filling the old winepress vat with water meant many trips to the standpipe, running and laughing, splashing and spilling the precious water on clothes and bare feet in a spirit of hilarity and competition, counting the number of runs each child could tot up. But help from adult-assistants soon filled the container. The brick maker fetched two moulds for the procedure. A brick mould is made of two parallel planks of wood, with sections between them to accommodate a builder's ordinary brick. It has to be immersed in water before use to prevent the mixture sticking to the sides.

A clay mound is first constructed, like a child's sandcastle. Water and straw are added, using a spade, and the ingredients are mixed to a setting consistency. The mixture looks like a gargantuan hedgehog, with spines radiating in all directions. This, of course, presented no deterrent to children; we couldn't resist planting a foot in, to squelch in the mud.

"Keep away, you diavolakia (little demons), or you'll get your toes chopped off!" So the exhausted worker would angrily warn us.

The moulds are prepared and positioned on a flat surface to ensure the uniformity of the bricks and set in the full glare of the

36

sun. Spadefuls of clay, striated with straw, are emptied into them. The excess muddy liquid is removed by shaking the moulds to and fro on their firm base. The newly made mud bricks are then left to bake in the fierce heat of the summer sunshine.

Once the bricks were ready, our father set to work according to his own careful drawings, and the result was very much what an embryonic Aga must have once looked like. He built it against the north wall of the house. Its length was that of two dining room chairs side by side, the width just one chair. Only four people could sit by it at a time. Its height was up to the seat of the chairs, but in our multifunctional kitchen, it was such a comfort.

It was fired by wood, and just as our father had predicted, generated a lot of energy for cooking and heating water. It made life so much easier for of us. Our father was justly proud and so was all the family.

Unfortunately, our embryonic Aga had to be removed; its weight was too great for the floor suspension to bear. After all the hard work putting it together, it had to be taken down brick by brick. A very great disappointment indeed and a return to cooking meals in the old burdensome way. Nonetheless, our father was an innovator, and one who enjoyed his frequent successes, but who accepted his failures with much less grace and fortitude. He made, for example, a wool-spinning machine, on the principle of our mother's Singer treadle sewing machine. He could be relentless in pursuing ideas until he accomplished his project. He constructed an appliance with wood and some metal. Using a short length of dowling, he made the horizontal body, similar to a sewing machine; a vertical structure contained the driving wheel and belt. He inserted a metal nozzle to be the main part of the structure, in order for the spun wool to go through and be wound over it. The top part was then fixed to the table and was attached to the larger wheel under it in order to activate the one above. Thus, the machine was ready. All the operator had to do was to use the footplate and synchronise hands with feet.

I cannot now remember the actual details. What I do remember, however, is sitting at the innovation and spinning. I wound a length of white-carded wool over my left arm, starting from the elbow to the wrist. Then to start spinning, I had to connect with the machine. A length of string protruded from the nozzle to give me anchorage. I pulled a few wisps of wool from the coil on my wrist, twisted it into a little yarn and attached it to the string with a secure knot. With fingers and thumbs, I began to ease and feed the wool into the hungry mouth, although synchronising hands with feet was very difficult and frustrating: the yarn kept snapping off because my feet had less to do than my hands. The hungry mouth of the nozzle kept gobbling up the yarn too fast for my immature dexterity. It looked so easy and so effortless when Mamma was spinning–I may have been my mother's daughter, but I was nowhere near her equal. I did eventually succeed, however.

Back then, there were no toys to buy for children. It was our father who once designed a scooter for our little brother, Byron. The Greeks treat Lord Byron as a great Philhellenic hero and sometimes (even offending their relatives!) name their children in his honour. A different name, Valsamis, the name of our deceased maternal Grandfather, was the original chosen name, but when the priest asked what was the child to be called, our father, towering over the congregation, cried out "BYRON Valsamis!" Grandma was offended: her feelings were hurt that her beloved husband's name was to come second to a foreigner's. Yet, to ensure the perpetuation of that noble name into the future generations of our family, Byron has called one of his own grandsons after Lord Byron, too.

The scooter proved a great success. It was a lot of hard work because all of the materials had to be sourced and hand-prepared, and our father had to do all of it himself. But the result was an entirely unique scooter, an ingenious prototype in our world! Lucky boy, Byron! Congratulations, Iraclis!

Talking of our father's more ambitious schemes, as well as scooters and bicycles, I also remember a bicycle journey. By bicycle he would go to the island of Ammoliani about 5 kilometres from Ouranoupolis. Most of the village people came to watch and jeer, for no one believed it would ever be possible.

That day was an eventful one for our family. One of our precious egg-laying chickens gave up the ghost, according to Grandma, for no apparent reason. And that was bad news on at least two counts. It was always sad to lose a creature we looked on as a pet, but it was also a loss of a provider for our already exhausted food supply.

The second event that day was much happier and exciting: an expectant mother! Our goat, Pipitsou produced twin kids. I saw the birth with my own eyes. The newly born goats looked wet, dazed and surprised, as Pipitsou licked them clean and dry. They wobbled a few times, but were soon able to stand up. How quickly and firmly they attached themselves to the milk sack.

Our father, of course, had other business. He planned to cross the water 5 kilometres to Ammoliani. He had adapted his ancient bicycle with paddles. What other changes he made, I cannot remember. All I really know is that the attempt was not successful. He had to turn back. Many curious lookers-on had a laugh at his expense. They never believed he could make it anyway, not with his so-called clever contraption. He dismissed them all, referring to them as a "jealous lot, envious of his enterprise."

My father however, is my present subject, so let me recall my father's workshop: a long, low stone building, similar in construction to the great Tower. It had two high windows, or maybe I was too young to look out of them because they were out of reach. However, I thought of them as very tall. The monks may well have used the building as an arsenal for their fishing boats or for storage of wood and animal feed before the Greek government annexed it in 1923. It had a wide door that opened out onto the square, just in front of the Tower. Where the workshop once stood, today there is now an open space with a water fountain. I feel sad each time I pass by; the workshop was another unique feature destroyed by the authorities of that time.

Our father worked with his own father, though only occasionally. Grandfather Yiannis was a skilled cooper and was able to turn his capable hands to any work requiring his bag of carpentry tools. For us and for anyone else who asked, he would make wooden clogs; shoes were out of reach for many people of our village. In the summer, they made a great noise on the baked earth, and in the winter, we sank and got stuck in the muddy roads, arriving home with our clogs heavy with the cloying mess.

Our Grandfather Yiannis had a great sense of humour. When

the first tractor finally made it to our village, he greeted it with an armful of hay for feeding. Once, when he passed a neighbour and asked after her health, she said, "Leave it, Yiannis, leave it," whereupon he dropped his tool bag and began to walk away. "Yiannis, Yiannis, you left your tool bag!"

"Didn't you tell me to leave it? So I left it!"

I possess an item that once belonged to our grandfather. Like all Greek men, he used the traditional komboloi, known as worry beads. They are lustrous agate stones; most of them are deep red and a few are black. My youngest brother, Yiannis, appropriated them. Ultimately, I persuaded him to let me have them. I converted them to a necklace, and I think of our kind grandfather each time I clasp it round my neck.

Our father was a carpenter and furniture maker. No one in our village had any money to speak of, but fortunately, Mr. and Mrs. Sydney F. Loch were newly arrived in our village in 1928 having served in the First World War, and subsequently, later, in the Second World War, as relief workers with the Quakers. They rented the Tower from the Greek government and turned it into their home. Of course, it needed repairs throughout and a good deal of furniture, to make it habitable, so father and son were employed there for many months, working for the Lochs, and their labours were often called upon as needs arose. The Lochs really became the saviours of us all. Sydney Loch was my own particular saviour, as you will see, and I will elaborate later on his contribution to my life.

The smell of wood shavings—at any time, no matter where—transports me at once back to my father's workshop: I am a small child again, sent to fetch off-cuts and shavings for the kitchen fire. I am shuffling barefoot and almost knee-high in wood shavings and sawdust between my toes. I am bending down here and there, picking up small off-cuts of wood and shavings to carry home in my little cane basket. Those memories are endless and persistent in my thoughts.

Fish glue had a strong ammonia smell that pervaded not only the workshop, but also the entire square, and clung to one's clothing. I disliked it; yet, in time, it no longer repelled me as fiercely as it once did.

40

I remember a particular conger eel. It had been opened up from the mouth to its tail, eviscerated and filleted. The monster, we were warned, could snap our arms or legs if we waded in its vicinity. Its lair had been in the submerged rock, just below the Tower, but now it was reduced to a triangle: stretched out and kept taut with a wooden spike at its widest end. It looked like a cravat hung out to dry. But before the final humiliation of the fearsome conger eel, coarse salt had been rubbed into its pristine white flesh and horribly mutilated to enhance the salinity. Rigani, an organic herb, handpicked from Athos boundary, had been added, too, to compliment the taste and defy the flies to colonise it. The eel had been suspended on a line to be cured by the summer's intense air temperature and direct sunlight. I remember my father and Mitsos, his part-time helper, sitting down in the workshop to eat the eel as a meze, a Turkish word meaning a starter, with real relish, accompanied by a home-distilled ouzo—dare I repeat 'organic'?—for certainly it would have been. The grapes, after pressing, had their skins distilled. The result was an occasion for celebration. That liquid would have been 100-proof. Many a time I recall our mother making use of it as an antiseptic for cuts and grazes, and oh boy, how it did sting!

The workshop had this relaxed and intimate atmosphere, resting when tired, eating the odd meze when available. Pickled olives and salt fish were usual alternatives, all meals and snacks accompanied, of course, by home-baked coarse bread. It was from here that our father embarked on realising his ambitious dream—to build a boat big enough to carry many passengers to the islands across the sea from our village. He was determined to accomplish this labour alone, like Hercules of the Greek myths, after whom he was named.

The first model boat was a solid block of wood carved in the shape of a little boat only two metres long. It was marked in squares with numbers, and to our great disappointment, our father cut through the markings, reducing the solid item to so many tiny pieces. To our incessant questionings, his reply was simply, "Wait and see. Be patient."

The model was made using his drawings on the bedroom floor. Dissecting the large pieces was like the use of graph paper to enlarge an end product. And he did succeed in building a small vessel, adding sails. We then went to the seaside, with a lot of village sceptics, to watch the launch. Even now I feel a frisson of excitement and fear, just in case our father failed to sail away to Ammoliani. Yes, he rolled up his trouser legs, put one foot in the quatro, pushed the earth hard away with the other, and with both legs well planted on board, he stood up in triumph and promptly navigated his way to Ammoliani! Everyone cheered and applauded: our family more than the rest of them.

But this was just the beginning.

In our paternal grandfather's field were pine trees, which father decided were suitable for his purposes. He undertook single-handedly to fell them. He must have toiled with an axe for many hours, cutting down the giants one by one. He worked so hard felling the trees and preparing them to convert them into timber for his 'real boat.' The smell of the resin evokes for me so many memories, especially of my visits to take father his lunch. Resinated wine, however, is still not to my taste.

My father's saw was like the capital letter H without the horizontal line. Both ends were blocked with thick, twisted rope. In the centre of each end, father inserted into the twisted ropes the vertical saw, which shone and glinted in the bright sunlight, displaying in its entire length shark-like teeth of huge proportions. I remember him shifting a prepared tree for sawing, securing it on a giant Y-stump, then, grasping the saw with his large powerful hands, carefully beginning the seesaw action, until the sharp teeth sank deeply into the wood. As he pulled and pushed, the tree's life poured down to the earth as sawdust on the green grass, and the sweat on father's brow ran in rivulets down his unshaven face. I looked on in awe; only his breath forced out at each push forward broke the monotony of the rasping noise of sawing.

Father insisted on preparing all the wood himself, so it seemed to take forever, and we began to lose our enthusiasm for the project. He was always sawing, shaping, planning, gluing. He made his own glue. He would boil fish skins and bones for what seemed hours, and the workshop would be filled with the most foul and nauseating smell. We kept well away until it evaporated.

When was he going to start building the boat? All we could see was a pile of planks in one corner, a lot of bent pieces of wood in another, while he continued to work with his plane, producing silky wood shavings we never tired of gathering into the basket.

Then, one day, we saw the skeleton of a boat before us, and we began to get a sense of all his great efforts. He had failed to communicate with us during his work; perhaps he just thought us too young to understand. Patience, however, was never one of his virtues. He was too intimidating. He rarely encouraged any dialogue with us. As a father, he was a hard man. I recall that he made us very upset and jealous on one occasion by refusing to make a pair of clogs for our young brother, yet presenting a fine pair to another boy outside our family. He announced that it was "to teach his son a lesson," though I cannot recollect what lesson that was.

At long last, the great boat began to take shape. Father painted it himself, which was arduous work and had to be repeated several times in different colours. We were curious about the name that would appear. Would it be Mamma's or one of our sisters'? Or even one of our brothers? Might he name it after me? I was his first-born, though being a girl could prove disadvantageous. What a disappointment it was, instead of my name, his own, Iraclis was emblazoned on both sides of the prow.

He did take us and our friends on the maiden voyage, to the islands opposite, and that was exciting. We were proud of our father's accomplishment and brushed aside our disappointment at the naming. On the return trip, the engine failed—a bad omen. But we were halfway to the shore, the sea was calm and clear, and we enjoyed staring down into the deep. We saw fish, rocks, seaweed, even, we imagined, the submerged Dion city wall stretching from our village across to the island Iraclis sailed to Thessaloniki eventually, with father as the captain, and spent many seasons taking people off on afternoon outings. Our father Iraclis was more than happy, sailing in his creation and enjoying a life away from his large family.

THE SOLDIER

During the war, in the summer of 1940, a child passed our front door, crying hysterically. We sprang out of the house followed by our mother, who attempted to reassure the distraught child and find out the cause of her distress. Ioni, the young girl, went every day to take some lunch to her father, who slept in the open, out in his field, to deter the wild boar from spoiling his vine crop. On this particular morning, she had found him stretched out on the ground, apparently sleeping, but she couldn't rouse him. What especially distressed her was a large piece of meat on his chest. At least, that was what she said it looked like.

He was eventually brought to the village on a wooden ladder: This was the only way of moving the sick and the dead. The priest announced the death by ringing the church bell in a mournful toll, and at that sound, the village population ran out of their homes to find out who had expired. By the time the victim passed our front door, the crowd had swelled to ever greater numbers, following his progression to his final destination: his home.

I too rushed forward to join the throng of other children. I was eager to get a closer look as that ladder and its load were lowered to the ground in front of the grieving family. We squatted on our haunches to get a good look at the supposed "meat" on his chest, but there was nothing of substance on him, just congealed blood extending from his neck to his waist. We lost interest.

What caught my attention, though, was a row of highly polished black shoes, seen between the legs of the crowd from my hunched position. As my eyes travelled upwards, the shoes climbed up the legs and became knee-high boots. Onwards and upwards, the boots ended in legs covered by grey trousers, and then grew into full-grown men in uniforms, with belts, shiny buttons, and peaked caps. I had never seen anything like this before. All of these grand accoutrements on tall blond men; my very first encounter with German soldiers. In fact, they were all German officers of some rank. I do not recollect their verdict on the events that had transpired in the dead man's field, but I know now, many decades later, the reason for their presence.

A British fighter plane had landed in a field within a kilometre of the village. I remember seeing it with other children, burnt out and empty. There was no talk of survivors, so we were told. I believe now that there were, and they were hiding in a safe place. The Germans had a suspicion British officers were in the vicinity on their way to Athos, waiting to escape. How right they were, and how fortunate we were, children then, that we had no idea that our own father had rowed the British along the coastline to the Holy Mountain, under the cover of darkness and guided only by the stars. The safe housing of the two enemies, in fact, took place in the same monastery that housed these German officers, eating and drinking the monks' food and wine, happily singing. All the while their British counterparts celebrated in silence, relaxed, up above their heads in the loft!

THE MATRIARCH

I cannot recollect now at what age I finally realised that our Grandmother was not the mother of all, the mother of all the people of our village. We were a team, my Grandmother and I. By the time I reached the age of nine (when Mamma gave birth to a fifth child), I considered myself one hundred years old. I felt so tired and aged because of the many, so it seemed to me, tasks constantly assigned to me to perform. But my grandmother always remained a friend.

My memory of our grandmother, looking back now, is of an old lady of medium height, slender and always slightly bent. Her hair was pure white, worn in a bun at the back of her head. Her eyes were blue and kindly. Her cheeks were furrowed and her facial skin was lovely and soft. She always wore black or grey clothes, because for as long as I can properly remember, my grandma was a widow. I have no recollection of her dressed in colourful garments. Widows in villages wear black to the end of their days and seldom remarry, even today.

She was always kind and uncomplaining, though I did hear her once saying to my mother that our parents had managed to ruin her marriage. This signified nothing to me at the time, however. I discovered later that when the twins had been born one November, which marked the beginning of a bitterly cold winter, I actually had to share my grandparents' bed. I understood this much more as an adult.

I remember her so well, and yet, I didn't know everything about her. It was a great surprise to me when I discovered that our grandmother was an only daughter, much adored by her very well-to-do parents, and much admired by all for her beauty and gentle disposition as a young woman.

But that was far back, before she came to our village.

As a child, I had only the barest understanding that my life in Ouranoupolis was merely the tip of an iceberg of epic dispossession. Our maternal and paternal grandparents, and their parents and grandparents before them, back for many generations, had not lived in Greece but on the Princes Isles, in the Sea of Marmara, in Asia Minor, which we now call Turkey. My grandparents, before they came to Greece, were part of well-established families with good businesses, coexisting amicably with the Turkish people, many of whom were employed by the Greeks.

It was in 1918 that they were forced into exile twice by the Turkish government. Their goods and property were confiscated; they left with only what they could load onto carts. My maternal grandmother's own mother died en route during the second exile. For my paternal grandmother, the loss was even more tragic: Her baby and a toddler also died on the way to the interior of Turkey. They were forced to walk on, despite the deaths, and it wasn't until they stopped at a tiny hamlet that a Turkish woman helped my distraught grandmother bury her children at the roadside. My heart goes out now to all refugees, whatever their ethnicity, because first and foremost, they are all human beings, not political pawns. Exile can be such a terrible thing.

Let me invite you now to the proceedings of my maternal grandmother's formal engagement, back on the Princes Islands —a place and a world she knew so well, but which I never had the fortune to experience. I was not even aware of the dowry I will disclose to you—not until just a few years ago. It was in the possession of my sister Angeliki who quite forgot to tell me of its existence.

The betrothal ceremony took place in 1895. One of my own granddaughters was born one hundred years later, and to her I will give the framed copy of the ceremony: Her middle name is Evgenia (Eugenie) in honour of our Grandmother Evgenia.

The content of the document is loosely translated from the Greek and reads as follows:

As at the Wedding in Canaan, where Jesus turned the water into wine and sanctified the marriage with God's blessings, so in the traditional Orthodox way we too, like all who were present then, ask for such a blessing on our daughter, Evgenia.

We, Avgerinos Vlastis and my wife Yiassimi, give our daughter, Evgenia, to be the wife of the noble Valsamis Konstandinou.

We give Evgenia our blessing and wish her long and sustained happiness in her life.

We bestow upon her the following dowry:

1 icon of the Virgin Mary with gold embroidered runner costing 2 guineas

4 mattresses, one stuffed with wool. 5 silk embroidered bedcovers. 10 duvets.

12 pairs of sheets, 5 of them in silk. 6 blankets, 2 of them in wool. 32 cushions, 10 of them stuffed with wool for use on the settee. 20 pillows, 7 with silk embroidery and beads for use on the settee.

70 nightshirts, 3 of pure silk. 4 petticoats . 25 dresses, 8 of pure silk.

15 tablecloths, 12 silk serviettes, 50 towels in linen of various sizes, 4 edged with lace.

7 handkerchiefs edged with gold lace. 3 tobacco pouches, 2 with gold thread embroidery.

1 watch case embroidered in gold thread. 3 coats in wool silk and cashmere costing 3 guineas.

3 silk blouses, 1 dress in taffeta at 3 guineas, 1 velvet dress, and 1 golden guinea. 10 silk shawls.

16 head scarves, 1 silk embroidered handkerchief at 1.5 guineas. 60 embroidered body belts.

2 nightdresses, 1 in broderie Anglaise, 1 in silk. 8 pairs of stockings.

12 handmade lace curtains. 3 pairs of handmade lace bed covers. 2 silk clothes bags. 2 face towels, 1 in silk. 1 kilim at 2 golden guineas. 2 candlesticks, 2 kettles. 3 casseroles, 1 baking dish. 1 room warmer, 1 luxury trunk at 1.5 guineas.

1 vineyard, 1 vat for treading the grapes, 1 barrel of wine, 1 farm.

20 Turkish golden guineas.

From the bride's mother to her daughter:

1 pearl, 5 sovereigns, 30 golden Venetian guineas, 1 pair of earrings at 1.5 gold sovereigns, 1 gold ring and a sewing machine.

From the groom to his bride to be:

1 diamond ring at 5 guineas, 1 gold wrist watch at 5 guineas, an outfit of clothes at 5 guineas, 1 fur coat at 5 guineas, 200 golden Turkish guineas.

From the Groom's father to the couple:

1 diamond ring for the Groom at 3 golden sovereigns, 1 vineyard, a bakery, 200 golden Turkish guineas.

We the parents bestow the above to our children, Evgenia and Valsamis, and may God grant them health, unity and peace throughout their lives.

In the year of our Lord 1895.

The signatories to the ceremony were Evgenia and Valsamis, the parents of the couple, the registrar and his deputy, and seven witnesses. Such a betrothal was an official document: it had a Turkish stamp to demonstrate its authenticity, even though the participants were all Greek nationals.

God did indeed grant them health, wealth, and unity: They produced three daughters and lived together in peace, but only for twenty-five years. They were exiled then, not once, but twice. They suffered from illness, poverty and tragic loss of loved ones. Survival suddenly became the operative word, and their long odyssey through life had only just begun. In 1923, they returned to Greece, first in the Peloponese where life was in a house shared with three other families. They were allocated one room for five adults, with the use of a shared kitchen and some minimal washing facilities. Then, in 1928, they were removed for the last time and placed on the arid granite soil of the village we came to know as Ouranoupolis.

My Godfather

Sydney Frederick Loch was a Scotsman. According to my godmother, Joice M Loch, his wife, he went to Australia at the age of seventeen to start a new life. He worked as a jackaroo on several sheep stations to earn a living and gain experience of life in practical isolation. He lived alone; his only companions were his two dogs. He shared nature with all the other creatures his host country produced. Sydney bought land, worked laboriously to clear it, but the whole thing simply wasn't to be: Gallipoli intervened.

He joined the Australian Volunteer Force and went to war. According to Joice Loch, my godmother, Sydney Loch developed typhoid towards the end of the campaign, but he was wounded before he could report it. My future father-in-law, A.J. White, a Londoner, was recruited at much the same time, even though he was only sixteen years old. He survived the war but was severely shell-shocked in the process.

Sydney Loch, my future godfather, kept a diary recording the horrors of that campaign. He eventually presented the contents as a novel under the title, "The Straits Impregnable" by Sydney De Loghe; the pseudonym was in order to avoid censorship by the Australian military, which feared the publicity would reveal the truth. Sir John Murray published it in 1917. The banned account of Gallipoli by Sydney Loch, "To Hell and Back," by Susanna De Vries, is now in its third edition. It is an in-depth account of his parentage, his childhood and his innumerable achievements.

Sydney and Joice Loch, his wife, worked in journalism in Ireland at the time of great hostility to the British regime. On arriving in England, they joined the Quakers to assist the Poles during the outbreak of the First World War. Sydney helped with reconstruction, and Joice immersed herself in welfare. In 1923, they visited Greece and discovered what was to be our village—the village of Prosphorion (meaning gift), renamed Pyrgos because it is dominated by a tower (pyrgos). The village is known today as Ouranoupolis (The Heavenly Sky/City). The new habitations there were being prepared for Greek refugees arriving in 1928 from Asia Minor, which is now Turkey.

The Tower was ancient, built by Andronicus the Second about eight hundred years ago. The Lochs fell in love with it and made it their home, spending a good part of the year amongst the village people, who by 1928 had been settled there from Turkey. These were the families who had lost all their goods and money and were now subjects of abject poverty.

Sydney and Joice Loch became the bringers of hope and much-needed relief in various ways. Joice, who later became my godmother, was the medic: she had acquired her skills growing up in the Australian outback. Sydney was her escort and interpreter in the village, as Joice never mastered the Greek language. They often visited the sick, both day and night. I retain a vision in my mind of my godfather holding up a hurricane lamp to show my godmother the way along those blind roads.

Many friends visiting the Lochs were asked to contribute to the medicine store: from pills to potions, and bandages, Elastoplasts etc. I remember a pleasant iodine smell every time Joice raised the lid of the medicine chest, one of the many items of furniture made by my carpenter father and grandfather.

People would arrive at the library/sitting room at all hours of the day and night to have their injuries and sores treated by Joice, who was always busy typing articles for Blackwood's Magazine. She would daub Gentian Violet with a piece of cotton wool on cuts and sores. Young patients became marked individuals, displaying their colours with pride, like badges of honour. Joice became an expert at sewing up skin lacerations using surgical needles (already threaded—generously donated by the British Navy in appreciation of the Loch's hospitality). I remember an incident, often repeated, about the youth who was brought to the Tower during the night. A fight had left him with a gaping injury to his scalp. The Lochs were there; my godfather would have held up the oil lamp to enable my

51

godmother to sew up the tear.

Joice, my godmother, refused to give injections or deliver babies: She feared being taken to court if adverse reactions or complications developed due to her intervention, since she was not a Greek. However, years later, on my first visit to Greece after an absence of nine years in 1959 she ordered me to attend a young woman in labour. My protestations about the lack of instruments, gloves and the fact that the Royal College of Midwives, my union, would not have approved, were swept aside.

I found the patient on a mattress on the floor. Sitting beside her were the two lay midwives of old: one was reciting the Lord's Prayer, the other followed with the Creed. Between their seated selves was the Panagia's ever-flowering plant. I conducted the delivery without any pain relief for the labouring patient, in bare hands and without sterile supplies necessary for this procedure. I did get the prospective grandmother to boil her best scissors and a length of string, however. Thankfully, the outcome was successful: both mother and baby were well. The entire village echoed the good news. From then on, each time I was visiting home, someone seemed to be waiting for me to attend the delivery. I was even called out during my honeymoon!

I think it is worth saying a few words about my first patient in Ouranoupolis: she was the second choice my godfather had made as his godchild, but her parents did not approve of a non-Orthodox person being spiritually connected with their baby girl. Had she been the goddaughter, I might well have been the patient, and she the midwife.

But, I digress and will return to where I left off.

In the summer of 1932, the British Navy was on exercise in the Mediterranean Sea. The captain visited the Lochs and learnt the plight of the people. In commiseration, he left a few medical supplies to augment Joice's arsenal; however, when the ship returned to deeper water by Mount Athos, the radar alerted him to an imminent earthquake in the area across the peninsula from our village. Instead of carrying on to their next destination, they returned to Ouranoupolis, informed the Lochs of the earthquake site, turned about, rounded the Holy Mountain and arrived at the village of Erissos to find it in darkness and almost flattened. They disembarked with life-saving supplies: pain relief and wound dressings, including sterile instruments and threaded needles. The Navy was eventually joined by the Lochs and some young men from Ouranoupolis, my father amongst them, helping with first aid and remaining at Erissos until the Red Cross and the Greek Army arrived. My father would often relate that horrifying experience. He was full of praise and admiration for the enormous contribution made by the British Navy. He spoke of how the sailors baked bread daily for the survivors and the helpers, and how they provided drinking water, as it was September, a hot month, and so very critical to the survival of those poor people. As a carpenter, my father was able to appreciate the construction of temporary but essential outbuildings in which the injured were placed. Those able sailors built latrines to such a high standard that the police wanted them for their offices!

The Lochs became our saviours. Many of us would not have survived but for their care and the financial support from their own small income earned through journalism. They genuinely wished to be accepted by these desperately needy people and create a bond between them by becoming godparents to just two infants, with the ultimate aim of educating them.

Sydney Loch was the first to approach a family who had a baby boy.

"We are very sad," they said, "but no, many thanks—you are not of the Orthodox faith and also xenos—a stranger."

What a rebuff! But he did not give up and offered to be godfather to a baby girl. And Sydney Loch received the same reply!

He would try again; have another go, third time lucky? Oh, yes! For he had the father of his prospective godchild under his very own roof working for him...

Iraclis, my father, and his father, Barba Yiannis, were carpenters. My father made many items of furniture in the new Loch residence.

"Iraclis, is there another new baby in the village who is not yet christened? I would like to be the godfather."

"We have one!" replied my father.

"What do you say to my proposal then Iraclis?"

My father accepted with no hesitation and without consulting my mother, because an Englishman was a persona grata as far as he was concerned. To him, it was a great honour to be associated with a man who was connected with Lord Byron of Messolongi, a hero to Greeks.

In fact, my father named one of my brothers Byron, who is also an admirer of the poet and has a grandson of the same name.

I was christened in the Tower chapel, the first time ever the Holy Family and Saints gazed on a naked female infant being immersed in the font! Other parents would not climb to the chapel with their babies, fearing another earthquake, which had caused just a little damage to the building. The chapel was small and intimate, a replica of an Orthodox Church. On the floor is a tile with the double-headed Eagle of Byzantium. My own husband copied it and made a plaque for our porch in Ouranoupolis and one for the Chapel in the cemetery. I have also embroidered the design on cushions.

I feel honoured and privileged to have been baptised in such a unique and consecrated place. Becoming Sydney Loch's godchild and receiving his name was a great honour. I was also given a Christian name to comply with the tenets of the Orthodox Church: Evangelismos, good news. The angel Gabriel greeted the Virgin Mary, telling her the good news: that she would produce Jesus, the son of God. This event is alleged to have occurred on March 25 and I was born on March 24; it was therefore appropriate to give me the Christian name of Evangeline–good news for my parents.

Joice became my godmother automatically by her marriage to Sydney Loch, but she was also a real godmother in her own right: She was accepted by the first family she approached. Ellie was duly christened in the village church; however, her parents could not be persuaded to let her go away. Ellie did not have much contact with her godmother. Sadly, Ellie passed away in 2009.

My godfather was my best friend. He was also my saviour. I have some precious memories with vivid images still in my mind. I remember being carried in his arms along the path leading to the library/lounge. The library was a vast rectangular room: it had a high ceiling, the floor stretched along way to the west windows facing the island of Ammouliani. There were windows on both sides. This room is part of the museum; therefore, the windows are blocked out in order to protect the excavated treasures from natural light.

My godmother would be found seated at her desk (made by my father), her back to the west window, typing. Her articles were published in Blackwoods Magazine. I possess two copies: March 1935 and February 1958.

My Godfather worked upstairs, in the adjoining building to the Tower. The guest bedrooms were along the landing but their private quarters were in the two rooms facing south, in what is now part of the museum.

Sydney Loch would also be hard at work on his typewriter, unless of course, he was drawing pictures of animals for me.

Their combined income provided water on stand pipes, a school, a church and agricultural implements much in demand. My godmother also imported Chios sheep; they yielded much more milk than goats. Life was made easier; however, poverty persisted.

My Godmother in collaboration with a man from Caesarea who knew how to make rugs. Joice Loch started an industry for the village girls. Looms were constructed, wool dyed with onion skins, the root of heathers and the bark of trees and from other natural sources.

My Godfather brought designs from Mount Athos: they were copied on graph paper by my Godmother.

The looms were installed in the tower; the man from Caesaria was at hand to instruct the women and girls who for the first time were able to earn money. The work was excellent, but who would buy the end product?

Many friends visited the Lochs; they admired the work and were encouraged to place orders. There was a market for the Pyrgos (Tower) rugs, so named because they were produced in Pyrgos

(before our village was renamed Ouranoupolis)

The workers were rewarded with well-earned money!

Eight of the Pyrgos rugs were removed from the Tower by the staff of the Archaeological Department of Byzantine Studies: my attempts to trace them have been unproductive.

But I have digressed and will resume at the point where I am in my godfather's arms. We were walking along the path leading to the library/lounge. There were lavender shrubs with tall roses behind them and big yellow butterflies with black lacy edging on their wings, flitting on and off around them. I would reach out to touch the trembling creatures, but they were too swift for me, much to my godfather's relief and amusement. On another occasion in the library, he picked me up, walked to the window where a big jar painted with large blue and pink flowers rested on the sill, and asked me to put my hand in it. Oh, yes—in went the small, eager hand that lost its way among the satiny treasures inside. I picked up a few tiny parcels but was told mono ena—one only! I then picked one sweet wrapped in shiny, pretty paper.

I remember the game when he would make sure I covered my eyes with my hands. He would then hide the sweet in a difficult spot and tell me to begin the search. He guided me with "hot" when I was near it and "cold" when too far away. I often interrupted his typing at the house, asking for a picture. He drew many little animals over and over again. He even played the guitar and sang to me.

I became aware of his concern and generosity for my welfare at an early age: he discovered that I was sharing a bed with my two sisters and grandmother, and he paid my own father to make a little bed for me. Now, I had my own bed. Yes, I was a very lucky child, indeed.

Then the war burst the bubble. Life would never be the same again for any of us. Within two years, another baby arrived. Despite my age, I became a part-time little mother at age ten! My godparents were in Cyprus at the time; it was a prolonged and traumatic separation. They were recruited once more by the Quaker Relief Service and went to Poland in 1939 until the end of the war. It was six years before their return in 1945.

GENESIS

We kept vigil, waiting for the mother to emerge for a short outing in order to have some much-needed sustenance and just a little exercise. Of course, she would be extremely anxious to return as undue delay could result in tragedy for her offspring. But this was the moment for us to move in fast.

We crept stealthily, very well aware that we were treading now on forbidden territory. Kneeling down by the nest, we would pick up one warm egg after another, listening for any movement, examining for tiny cracks, anything—anything that could signal our intervention.

"This one has a tiny crack!" whispered the one who held that particular egg to her ear, assuring us that it was already chirping. We believed, in our young little hearts and minds, that the little creature inside was actually asking to be released. Naturally, we felt that it was our duty to deliver the prisoner from such a constricting cell.

Little nimble fingers and rough nails eased up the edge from the cracked shell and began by peeling away enough to look inside. This uncovered a window with an opaque curtain. Actually, it was a bulging membrane. The impatient head with its sharp beak simply caused the protuberance.

No more help from us was necessary. The little beak punctured the bubble: a yellow head with two bright eyes blinked at the new world. The remaining walls of its home came apart at its departure. A wobbly ball of wet silk balancing on two stick-like legs, claws outstretched, gripped the floor of the nest amongst its still inert brothers and sisters. It was such a satisfying and exhilarating experience to be able to assist at the "birth" of a chick or two; we never tired of the opportunity. But we never risked waiting for that wet silkiness to dry because of the danger. We knew it was time for us to beat a quick retreat when we spied the mother's return. If we were caught at the site, she would become a tornado of beak, feathers and claws. Indeed, if my own Mamma had found out, the punishment would have been quite painful as well.

We had to contain our impatience until the mother hen brought her entire brood into the garden. She would cluck-cluck to them, and ten to twelve little golden balls of fluff would follow her, chirping away for the entire world to hear and welcome them. We looked upon them as our pets; yet, as they grew into adults, some of them had to be sacrificed, we knew, to provide a meal at Christmas, or when there was illness in the family. Chicken soup was the only nourishing food for invalids, after all.

LET THEM HAVE BABIES

We adored the tiny chirpy little balls of yellow fluff, but we had to admire them from afar: their mother would have scratched our eyes out and torn our hair had we got close. And Mamma would have offered no sympathy; on the contrary, she would have scolded us instead.

Grown-ups expected the hens to go on producing eggs throughout their adult life, without allowing for the urge to have any offspring. To that end, when a hen became broody, she was immediately imprisoned under a box in total darkness for many days, until that characteristic "cluck-cluck-cluck" was no longer heard. However, some of the ingenious creatures learned how to beat the system. After laying perhaps eight or ten eggs in a secret nest, they would sit on them. By the time the nest was discovered by us humans, it was too late to use the eggs for our family. Our reliance on the eggs as a source of protein was paramount, so it was very important to ensure that all the eggs for the next day were accounted for. But our chickens were simply anarchic and refused to follow our rules to not have babies.

During the spring and summer, they made wings for the acacia tree where they pecked at the foliage and the flowers before they quieted down and went to sleep. In the morning, the area below the acacia was entirely fouled and had to be swept before anyone could leave or enter the house because the tree was just outside the garden entrance to the home. Perhaps it was contempt for our attempts at controlling them.

In the autumn and winter, however, the tree was not appealing as an alternative to the coup. There they were huddled together to keep warm, yet would squabble and peck at their neighbours. The cockerel would eventually restore order, and sleep would maintain control. It was in this cramped and confined space that we had to make our rounds each day to find out how many eggs would be available for the 'morrow'.

Grandma would bend double to enter, with me reluctantly in tow. I had to be instructed in the procedure in case Mamma or Grandma was sick or unavailable to make the count. Grandma would place both hands gently on the slumbering body of the first hen, pick her up and hold her firmly under her left arm with the head pointing backwards.

Then came the part that made me want to retch: she would insert her middle finger into the hen's anus, feeling for an egg! She would check one bird after another in this way, thoroughly to the end of the row. I hated the procedure but knew it fell to me, as the oldest, to learn the art of egg counting.

The first time I performed the procedure, I expected the egg to be hard inside the hen, but it was soft. Exerting even a little pressure dented it. I expected to find that egg looking irregular in shape the next day when it was laid, but it was perfect. The experiment for me justified my involvement in a task I found revolting, yet one which had to be undertaken to guarantee the entire egg harvest for us.

The chickens always announced their performance loudly for us to hear and to come collect their offering. But where had they deposited it? To encourage them to use the appropriate place, a wooden egg was placed in each nest. But seldom did they lay their eggs in their purpose-fashioned nests inside the coup. If we expected four eggs but found only three in the coup, we had to go searching for that elusive fourth.

It was fun for us children trying to locate the egg. It was like the hunting for Easter eggs children nowadays do every year. A thick hedge separated our home from the church; often, a hen would find a spot that took her fancy and sit on it, listening to the liturgy and enjoying the doxology while she produced her own offering. Blessed were those offspring to us children, but for the adults, hens breeding when they weren't supposed to, caused them disappointment and dismay.

Murder Most Fowl

Mavroula is the diminutive for Mavry; it means "black." And she was black and beautiful. A working pet like our goats, she provided us with our eggs. Her head was adorned by a red lacy comb; her eyes were like two amber beads set within red circles and painted white on the periphery. Below them were two white dots the size of peas, and further down were two wattles, red and floppy. She had yellow legs with black feathers running down the side like spats. Her feet, too, were yellow, with curved talons for scratching the earth to find those choice bits to eat.

She was a glossy raven black; her plumage shone and shimmered iridescent in the sunshine. Mavroula was quite plump. Sadly, though this was a good sign for the laying of eggs, when she ultimately failed to produce them, it led her straight to the guillotine. Like starving humans, she was simply full of fluid; but unfortunately, we were not aware of that until it was much too late to save her.

She walked with a sedate wobble and sang as she cast her eyes about for food. She was happy and contented in her ignorance. Her serenity, however, was soon shattered when the cockerel, testosterone-fuelled, landed on her back. That libidinous creature loved to pin her to the ground and peck at her comb to keep her submissive. Her vocal protestations fell on his deaf ears, but it warned her sisters that the heathen male was on a rampage.

We betrayed Mavroula, our pet hen. Myself in particular, for utterly selfish reasons. But then, I was only just a twelve-year-old girl and Easter was approaching. I needed a pair of red sandals. I wanted to sell my pet for a pair of red sandals: What an Iscariot I was! We had arranged a barter with a family of friends who lived across the water 5 kilometres away on the island of Ammoliani. After a successful chase around the garden, we caught the bewildered creature and imprisoned her in a cardboard box. The only times Mavroula was ever thus restrained were when she was in a truly broody phase—and broody was something Mavroula certainly was not on that fateful day.

We embarked in a tiny rowing boat and I kept the box by my side the whole journey. Mavroula was restless; she knew a plot was in place. She began pecking at the walls of her cell, and I interpreted this as a reproach to me for removing her from her home and companions. Still, I was feeling very excited at the prospect of those wonderful red sandals. I failed to show any remorse at all. Our friends, of course, were delighted to see such a fat fowl and made many funny grunting noises of appreciation. Upon having to hand over the beautiful hen, I accepted the sandals, which were yellow and not the promised red, with much guilt and little pleasure, not in the least excited any longer, seeing my pet in the arms of another. On the return journey home, I was crestfallen and rather subdued.

There were no telephones in the village; communication was by word of mouth. It was, therefore, a long time after that we received a message of complaint from our friends. They were demanding compensation—their pound of flesh—for they had been most disappointed: Our hen was eggless. In the end, they had done the next best thing to get their money's worth from our unproductive bird: They beheaded the beautiful Mavroula!

The poor creature was murdered so that they could feast on her, sink their teeth in her flesh and make lemon soup with her unfortunate bones. However, when the plucking of her plumage revealed a bloated but very skinny body, the friends were even more furious than ever. Once they had cut her open, it was obvious that poor Mavroula was full of fluid because, like many of us there in the village, she was hopelessly malnourished. She should have been allowed to die in the garden or at home in her coop.

As for the sandals, well, they were yellow, and I had wanted red, so I wore them only once. I can see myself still, walking on the far side of Church Square in those ugly yellow sandals, teary-eyed and dreaming of my beautiful Mavroula.

LITTLE BROTHER

We—the three little girls—were told a baby would be arriving soon, but the next thing I recollect was being there at our mother's bedside and gazing down at a naked infant with a thick coil of blue and white knotted rope on its abdomen, expressing surprise and fear that its genitals looked like so many marbles! It was the very first time I had seen an umbilical cord and also my first exposure to the male sex organs. I had a little brother, now, and was shown the difference between boys and girls. I was five years old.

It was the custom to offer a spoonful of jam to all persons admitted to the birthing chamber to see the baby. This was to make life sweet for all the family and the baby's future, a custom rarely practised now, as babies are born away in town today, far from the extended families and traditional ways. This may sound sad, but it is safer, both for mother and for baby.

Where was the proud father that day? I have no recollection of him being present.

For me, however, there was another first that day, in the care of the umbilical cord, after its separation from the placenta. Grandma fetched the tin in which was kept the pulverised coffee. A small square piece of clean linen was slit half way to the centre like a key-hole and placed on the baby's abdomen encircling the base of the shortened length of the umbilical cord. With a teaspoon, coffee powder was gently and carefully placed round the limp and now pale stump. The ends of the linen were folded over it, making it thus like a tiny parcel. The packet was secured with a band of linen, wrapped firmly round the infant's body.

I do not remember the baby being given a bath at this juncture. However, when he was eventually bathed, he was immersed in warm water, and to this was added a handful of coarse salt and an equal measure of joiner's nails: this was to ensure an iron constitution!

Next, the child was bound from top to ankles: A specially woven band, known as the faskia, with two ties at the end, was rolled-up like a bandage. The baby was laid flat; the band was placed at the top of its chest, level with the shoulders. Grandma then began deftly and firmly to unroll it over and under the infant, straightening his arms and legs as she proceeded to envelop and cocoon him, leaving only his feet exposed, and securing the band with the attached twin strings. Finally, Grandma placed him in a triangular sheet and wrapped him in it by picking up one end and placing it across the chest, well over the shoulder. She brought up the end of the triangle over the tiny pink feet, and with the other end of the wrapper, covered the baby's body completely.

The child was now ready. Grandma picked him up with her gentle hands and proudly offered her first grandson to her own daughter, who cradled him in the angle of her arm, close to her side. There he slept for forty days and nights. Mother and baby remained house-bound until they were churched on the fortieth day, as in St. Luke's gospel, Chapter 2, Verse 22.

All mothers slept with their newborn babies in those days, it was convenient for breastfeeding and keeping the infants warm. Keeping warm was a problem for all of us. I had not heard of hot water bottles, let alone electric blankets, so I could not at that time feel deprived of what I couldn't guess. Nor could I imagine that one happy day I would slip into a bed and enjoy its seductive warmth and comfort in a house of my own, boasting central heating, double-glazing, or that my hot water bottle, if I needed it, would have a fleecy cover. What bliss! Back then, our poor substitute for central heating was the mangali or the brazier:

Eventually, my little brother was put into his cradle, which was suspended from the ceiling in the kitchen. The swing-cradle we used was a rectangle of tough fabric attached to two long parallel poles, with two shorter lengths at each end. It provided a trough-like hollow where the baby fitted snugly and safely. A length of cloth rope, made with strips of fabric from old clothes, so much kinder to the hands, cut in strips and plaited like hair, was attached

64

at the foot end of the suspension to provide us with the means of swinging the baby to sleep without having to get up. According to Mamma, I insisted as a child on taking hold of that rope when I went to bed in my small bedroom adjoining the kitchen, where mother and baby slept. Even in my sleep, I would swing the cradle when the baby cried.

I have remained a very light sleeper to this day. When my own children were babies, I woke up immediately they began to whimper, even though they were in their own bedrooms, a legacy, I think, of my own childhood.

It was a childhood in which I learned much about babies.

In 1940, our mother went into labour for the last time. There had been no antenatal care: none was available. It wasn't therefore possible to make any plans in case of anticipated complications. Most fortunately, for the first time ever, there was a professional midwife, well known to our family, who lived a few kilometres away in Nea Rhoda.

Long before the baby was born, I remember spending a couple of days at her house. I had been puzzled by what looked like a string of pegs; they were solid except for their rounded heads, which had holes, so that the pegs could be strung out like a necklace hung to dry. My question as to what these were was answered simply with "clothes-pegs," but many years later, at least twenty, when I was working as a student nurse myself, I came across the so-called 'pegs' again. They were, in fact, cervical dilators. When inserted into the cervix, they became swollen by the secretions and dilated the cervix, allowing access to the uterus, forcing the neck of the womb open in order to remove any remnants after miscarriages.

For the women in the villages, who knew of no birth control and became pregnant every year, this professional midwife must have been a godsend.

Dinah, the midwife, arrived as soon as Mamma went into labour, and we, the children, were soon packed off to relatives, even though this was not at all the usual practice. Dinah had discovered that the baby was clearly presenting as breech. The labour was bound to be protracted and painful, without any pain relief for our mother. It was a time of great anxiety for my Grandmother, my father and all the close relatives who gathered to support and encourage my parents.

It seemed a long time before we met our new baby brother; we had no idea of what our dear mother had gone through. Even had it been explained to us back then, I doubt whether we really would have been any wiser to the trauma experienced by mother and baby.

The progress of labour had been very slow. When the feet were delivered, the baby had to be forcefully extracted, a process that took a considerable time. Our father held Mamma under the arms firmly as the midwife pulled the baby's feet with all her strength. It must have been like a tug of war between the father and the midwife. The infant, when he eventually emerged, was the colour purple, limp, and looked like a thin, long, rag doll, I was told. Dinah took mouthfuls of tsipouro, a homemade distilled spirit of 100-proof, and spat it as a spray over our brother's face in order to make him breathe, while at the same time, tossing him up into the air and letting him land on the bed. Eventually, he breathed and then cried, albeit weakly.

But what immediate postnatal care was available for our mother? There was no relief, even for after pains. Damage would have been considerable, surely, to the birth canal and to its exterior, after such a delivery, yet I doubt very much whether it was ever repaired.

How long, then, did it take Mamma to recover? I was far too young to understand the consequences or grasp the stages of our mother's return to her former state of health, which was already so poor. As a midwife and mother myself, years later, I was able to appreciate how much Mamma suffered. I feel deeply grateful to Dinah, the midwife: without her, undoubtedly, the outcome for both mother and baby alike might well have been disastrous.

The baby was normal and healthy. He became the favourite of both parents and caused not a little sibling rivalry in years to come. That weak, limp, rag-doll of a baby grew to be a strong, tall and handsome man with a lung capacity that enabled him to remain submerged without oxygen for more than a couple of minutes whenever he went fishing, even well into his fifties, to the anxiety of anyone who rowed him out to sea. And this was in spite of being a chain-smoker and his fondness for wine and spirits. Now, however, he looks and sounds much older than his years.

I helped care for the infant during only the first four years of his life, since I had left home by the time I was fourteen years old and gone away to school, to return for only three days after the first year and another year passed before I came home again once for just a few days. Three more years were to elapse before I saw the entire family, prior to my final departure abroad.

As a nine-year-old and the eldest of five children, I had to grow up fast and help take care of the latest arrival to join the family. I fetched the water from the well, lit the fire to heat it, and washed his nappies made from old pieces of bed linen. Washing them out of doors, in all weathers was easy in the summer, but in the winter, the cold and icy weather made my hands very sore.

I gave my little brother his bottle at night. I slept on the floor with him beside me. Mamma lay on the bed, her fitful sleep interrupted by asthma and bouts of paroxysmal coughing, gasping for her breath.

And my father, where was he? His mother and sister were tucking him up in bed, as if he were the baby, or the one who had sleepless nights filled with illness. They treated him like a child, instead of encouraging him to be with his young family. They made him welcome in their home, to escape his duties as a father.

This was wartime, when a blackout was enforced; the bedroom was like a dungeon anyway, even at the best of times. When the baby cried, Mamma woke me up and asked me to warm his milk. It was contained in an enamelled cup, which I held over the feeble flame of the wick as it poked its shrivelled head out of the oily lagoon of the glass globe in which it was housed. The sickly flame hardly lit the room, so even if the windows had not been curtained, no aeroplane flying overhead would have spotted us. I well remember Mamma warning me to keep my hand steady, so that no milk was spilt. What I don't recollect is actually pouring it into the bottle and feeding the hungry baby; I must have been half asleep in the process.

He proved a lethargic child, slow to speak. For a while, we even thought he might be dumb, although we needn't have worried, as he finally learned at the age of four. Once he did, there was no holding his tongue. At school, he demonstrated marked ability for foreign languages and successfully acquired enough Spanish and English to get by comfortably in those countries.

Despite my tender years, I felt very protective towards him. He had a high fever one summer, possibly malaria, but was sleeping on a platform that served as his bed, outside under the shade of the vine, where his mouth was open to the buzzing flies. I would sit beside him, doing my level best to keep those at bay, while relieving his hot face with compresses, for which I used an old piece of linen, steeped in a bowl of water and vinegar, wrung out and placed on his burning cheeks and temples.

The Swiss Red Cross arrived at one point to vaccinate us all in the village against smallpox. I took my little brother by the hand, and walked him to the centre. When it was our turn, I removed his white vest, which was soiled with flea-spotting exposed for all to see, not just by the foreign people, but by our neighbours too, who were also awaiting their turn. My embarrassment was overwhelming. I took it personally; I felt it was my fault and it should never have happened. But flea stains were permanent: There was no way that digested blood could be removed by homemade soap alone, and no other chemical was available to us. Nonetheless, it was as if he were my child and I the neglectful mother.

UNDER THE MULBERRY TREE

The mulberry tree was to be found three houses from the church steps, towards the west sea front. In the summer, it produced delicious fruit, known to us as moura; it has the richness of sugared rhubarb and the tartness of a cranberry. Before they are ripe, they are very hard and sour and taste like cardboard; even the chickens reject them. Ripe moura take on the colour of deep purple—almost black. They don't remain long attached to the parent tree. They fall to the earth like rain, to the delight of children and chickens: first come first served! We preferred to pick them off the tree because when the soft, juicy fruit fell to the ground below, it became gritty and dusty from the dry earth. Some boys shinnied up the tree and gorged on them; others jumped up and pulled down a branch: in that way, most of the moura were lost to them. But those of us beneath the tree gobbled them up, the escaping juice a tell-tale sign of our activities when we got home.

The mulberry tree was not common property; it stood about two metres by the garden hedge of a little house, and there it sits to this day. It belonged to the family of an elderly lady. She was dressed in the traditional widow's black from head to toe. Sitting on the dusty ground cross-legged just like a Buddha, near the tree to guard the fruit. She sat with her eyes open wide, yet she had no vision—she was totally blind. She relied on her acute hearing and a long stick to stop young thieves from plundering her treasure. So, she would sit there looking ahead of her, seeing nothing, but hearing all. She remained in that spot, alone all day long, even when the others were having a siesta. She looked so lonely. Now, as an adult myself, I remember her as a pathetic, desolate figure—dejected and rejected.

She would wield her weapon at random when she heard us

approach, but the stick seldom reached us. We dared not even whisper - we were silent - our voices muted. We were good children in that we didn't taunt or tease her, but we simply could not resist the temptation of the berries. However, there came a time when our little voices were heard loud and clear by all to hear, when we were brought together under the mulberry tree for more serious games than trying to thieve a few precious berries.

It was on one particular summer's day: a calf was slaughtered, and we were all forced to drink a teaspoon of the vile bile: a secretion from the liver which aids digestion It was deep, green and had a most bitter taste that lingered in the mouth, in spite of the rubbery jelly sweet we were offered as recompense. Just last year, I finally asked the widow's daughter the reason for it. She said it was to clear our systems and free us from fevers. However, there was little in our systems needing that treatment: our diet was poor, we consumed no fatty foods, only some olive oil, when we were not actually fasting for the Easter or the Pentecost celebrations. As for the consumption of meat, Easter was the only time when a little goat meat was eaten. The fevers, however, they never left us at all—not until the mosquitoes were finally eliminated throughout the village. This was achieved only when the stagnant water-holes were sprayed by helicopters with DDT, sometime in the mid-1940s by the Government.

All kinds of 'treatment,' however, were meted out to children in those days. Children were perceived by the adults to be tongue-tied to some degree; thus, in our village, as soon as the child could obey the demand to open its mouth, the tongue had to be properly freed from its base. "Lift up your tongue to the roof of your mouth and keep still," the nurse or parent would say. The operator would use a razor blade and cut the tiny fleshy anchorage. There would follow bleeding and tears—a very unpleasant mouthful to swallow. In the case of my little brother, it made no difference; he was four years old before he uttered a single word, despite the razor-blade assault: we thought he was mute for the longest time.

Another ritual we had to endure was the release of the thin membrane attached under the top lip to the corresponding gum, yet another bloody intervention. This was supposed to prevent us from getting jaundiced, but it was really the breakdown of our red cells, destroyed by the malarial organisms, every summer that made us look yellow and skeletal.

Katherine and Sophia, my cousins, and I were sitting by a big hearth enjoying the log fire. This was in the Americana's house. Her husband, known as the Americanos, had been to work in America and made a lot of money. On his return to the village, he showed his wealth by having a home built in a fashion that could only be described as a small castle. It was surrounded by a high wall and had a tall wrought iron gate that was kept locked most of the time. Its roof was flat; I remember being permitted to haul up our freshly made trahana (a winter food made with ground wheat boiled in goat's or cow's milk) to dry, unhindered by dogs and cats and other children. It was very good to eat. I liked being assigned to guard it from the birds, having a taste every now and again myself.

It was indeed a privilege to be invited within. Mrs. Americana was very plump and moved very slowly. She spent most of her time sitting on the veranda during the summer and by the fireplace in the winter. She had no children of her own and enjoyed our company. She was our Scheherazade, regaling us with adventurous and romantic tales, making them up as she went along. On one such afternoon, she offered ear piercing. It would make us beautiful, she told us, like the heroines of her stories. She wobbled out of the room returning with a needle, thread and scissors, resumed her seat by the fireside armchair and picked Katherine as her first choice. She spat on the ashes, picked up a speck and rubbed Katherine's ear lobe and waited for it to dry. With the thick needle and equally thick thread, she pierced the tender flesh in but a moment. She pulled through the length of the thread and tied it to look like a hoop. She cut off the remainder and proceeded likewise with the other ear-lobe, whilst my cousin's tears flowed freely but silently.

Sophia was the next to kneel at the Americana's feet; Sophia was in fact her goddaughter. She approached and knelt with some hesitation, but took her place nevertheless. She endured the ordeal more or less like her elder sister, but a few sobs escaped her. I reminded her of the incident in the summer; she assured me that she will never forget it. She added that the holes had closed up, after all that pain, just like mine had done. When my turn came to kneel, I was frightened after I had witnessed my cousins' ordeal but

71

went through with it, not daring to show my pain such that I would be thought of as a weakling. When I returned home with thread hoops through red ear-lobes, mamma was very cross indeed. Within a couple of days, my ears looked inflamed—they were infected. One ear was much worse than the other. In fact, Mamma feared it would fall off. A very painful procedure was the only solution. She cut the hoops and gently, but still very painfully for me, because they were firmly glued with dried up pus, pulled the threads out. It was fortunate for me that our mother had the ability to recognise problems and solve them on her own. Her quick intervention and good aftercare saved my ears and the Americana's reputation. This lady did not offer one word of apology; all she would say was that we "wanted our ears pierced" and she had but humoured us. Katherine and I were under eight years of age; Sophia was only about six years old.

Let me tell you though, the fate of the mulberry tree, under whose shade so much violence was done! The modern housewife of our village starts the day by sweeping the yard in front of her home. The mulberry tree presents a regular problem, of course. The leaves and the fruit have to be constantly removed and the sweeping bruises the moura and stains the ground. The children have more choices in today's world: Will it be ice lollies, ice-cream, sweets, chocolates, baklava or cadaifi? The moura are no longer in demand. Even the modern-day chickens cannot eat the fruit because their owners have removed them to the countryside to a superior semi-free range lifestyle. The much sought after fruit is now rejected and considered a nuisance. Sadly, the mulberry trees have lost their popularity and most have been cut down.

MIDWIFE

There was no midwife, no nurse or doctor in Ouranoupolis. Two village women took it in turn to provide the service for the local mothers-to-be. On my first visit back to the village, in 1959 after an absence of nine years, having become a trained nurse and midwife, I was asked by my godmother, Mrs. Joice Loch, to attend a delivery in order to assist those same two village midwives, who were also called upon frequently to lay out the dead. One of them, Anthi, was additionally responsible for the cleaning of the church. As a child, I remember her replenishing the oil and trimming the wicks of the glass globes, surrounded by brass chains, in front of the icons. She also swept the floor, raising clouds of dust from its earthy surface. Our mother discouraged us from watching Anthi, to avoid the inhalation of dust that so plagued her.

These women had no training; they learnt from experience and from their mistakes. Anthi was softly spoken and humble; maybe the Church environment had a soothing effect on her, which she in turn transmitted to her circle of friends and patients.

Not so with her colleague, Smaro, who was tall, well built, intimidating, loud, and full of bravado. She was unkind to her second husband, consigning him to the old stable for his sleeping quarters. I recall she took pity on me one day and promised to cure my infected eyelids. I remember the yellow crusting in the corners, and the pussy lining visible at the edges of my eyelids. It was revolting to look at and very uncomfortable upon waking, because I was unable to open my eyes: the lids were glued tightly shut and my eye-lashes were encrusted with dried-up yellow pus. Washing with cold water every morning took much time and effort to relieve the problem, and was only a temporary fix. During the day, the pus would simply continue to accumulate inside the bottom lid. To remove it, I looked in the mirror and placed the tip of my index finger at the inner corner of my eye near my nose, pressing down on the sticky string of pus and gently lifting out the offending yellow, wormlike matter.

One day, Smaro gave me a small bottle of a magic fluid to drip into my eyes. It worked like a miracle! But when the supply was exhausted, the infection returned just as aggressively as it had come about. I was very disappointed, yet full of hope because I firmly believed that Smaro would come to my aid again. But, no, her bottle was broken, the magic potion spilt. No use crying, but I wept anyway. My vanity and comfort were splashed upon her stable-floor. I lost my faith in her thereafter and never accepted anything from her again.

THE WHEAT HARVEST

"We plough the fields and scatter the good seed on the land."

It would be a poor, obstinate donkey, an ancient cow or a morose bull that pulled the plough, the animals protesting vigorously to the yoke. A full nosebag was the bait, which never failed to catch the available animal. Whilst it nose-dived into the feed, the ploughman slipped the harness over its head. During this part of life, we children played a very small yet significant part: We were the bearers of food and drink to the ploughman. I do remember intermittent visits with Mamma or Grandma to find out the status of new growth sprouting out of the earth and report on the appearance of weeds, which sometimes proliferated. This was blamed on adulterated seed, a common practice of suppliers to augment its weight and pay more for less gain.

The spring made a green sea filled with fields of growing wheat. And among those moving heads of wheat, the scarlet heads of poppies kept up the rhythm. This is a childhood memory, but one I could not fully have appreciated back then. Now, I find those faraway green fields of my childhood have shrunk. By June, the wheat would be ripe and ready for harvest. I remember an endless expanse of gold stretching before us to the horizon. Seeing it as an adult, I now realise our field wasn't that vast: it was barely four hectares. But I nevertheless have nostalgic memories of days spent helping to reap it.

The reaper and his helpers arrived armed with scythes and wooden bent mittens with elongated, hooked index fingers of various sizes. Family members and older children were encouraged to participate. I was given a small scythe and wooden mitten and was bidden to observe the method used by one of the men. I soon got the knack of it. Standing on the starting line, I extended my left arm and hand fully, and sporting the wooden mitten with the crooked index finger, I brought it forward, encircling an armful of wheat. With the scythe in my dominant hand, I swung it to my right, brought it forward, cutting the bundle gathered. Success! I became a little too confident, however, thinking I could compete with adults.

Working fast with a scythe was not for children. I directed the scythe to the level of my knees: a painful lesson for me. Fortunately, the injury was rather superficial and was treated with a heavy dusting of soil. What about tetanus? The extreme sun temperature actually sterilizes the surface of the earth. No infection developed; however, the scar on my knee was still visible many decades later.

Another common injury, which was extremely painful, was treading on a thorn. There is a weed—trivoli—whose round seedpods, when dry, are as hard if encased in wood. They are an earthy colour, and from their cylindrical bodies, they radiate three sharp, needle-like thorns. We trod on them frequently because they blended in so very well with the soil. It was easy to step on one, usually on the heel. The pain was excruciating; it was sickening and vile. It went deep and caused much bleeding. The injured party would hop along for help, screaming in agony, yet would let no one attempt to extract the offending invader. There were cries of, "Don't touch me, go away!" and it did hurt a lot as it was being removed. Though it had no barbs, it felt as though it did. It was sucked into the flesh; bleeding and more pain followed its removal. I can speak on this topic from bitter experience.

The reaped grain stalks were left in heaps on the ground until one of the men needed a rest from scything. He would make a length of wheat by taking two handfuls, joining them by twisting the ends together, then lay it on the ground and take a big armful from the heap to make a sizeable sheaf. He tied it and stood it upright. At the end of the day, the sheaves were assembled in the shape of a rick.

The soil burnt the soles of our feet as we went about the fields without footwear. Walking on stubble presented another hazard to our young feet. There were injuries; however, there was always the sterilised soil to salve them. I do not subscribe to this treatment now, however.

We liked harvest time. We enjoyed the freedom and the picnic snacks, and some of us did actually help the reapers amid our play. We also ran errands up and down the field, taking messages or refreshments to them.

It was during these times when we walked or ran through the wheat, parting the stalks to make a path, that we would get both a thrill and a fright. A sudden movement would reveal a lizard in great haste to avoid us, or a little field mouse gathering a small share of the harvest would get panicky at our approach and disappear at the speed of light. We recovered quickly from both these minor incidents. It was only the barely perceptible sound of a snake slithering away that made us scream in terror, "Mammakamou!" (my little mother) or "Yiayiakamou!" (my little grandma), whoever was with us on that day. We had good reason to be frightened; there were many sightings of vipers and grass snakes, and we would not take the risk of coming close enough to identify them.

The ants intrigued us. As soon as the picnic was placed on the ground and the bread was roughly cut, the uninvited guests would arrive singly from all directions. They were light brown in colour and were bigger than their industrious and well-organised cousins. They moved about swiftly, finding the bread crumbs and any other food light enough to carry home.

Our fellow Lilliputian workers were the indefatigable ordinary ants. They were busy in making provisions for the winter months. They, too, moved fast, carrying grains bigger than their own body weight. They marched head-to-tail in columns, negotiating a zigzagged route over the uneven terrain made by the plough. Their destination was the underground quarters to fill up their coffers. The lazy cicadas sang whilst the world of men and ants below them laboured in the sizzling sun. They reckoned we favoured the ants and allowed them to have a share of the harvest. Their monotonous song was actually a curse, directed to the humans. It went like this:

> *You reap, you thresh, Therizeteh, alonizeteh,*
> *You give to the ants, Ton mirminga, ton thineteh,*
> *To me you give not, Emena then me thineteh,*
> *You make no pita, Miah pita then me kanete,*

77

Bread for me,
May you die! Next too hronou na pethaneteh!
Harvest year!

We sang in chorus with the cicadas, keeping up the monotone, but with gusto!

The harvest over, next comes the threshing. None of us had any idea that there was such an implement as a threshing machine: a mechanical means for separating the grain from the chaff. Instead, man and beast on dusty ground, and at the whim of the weather, achieved it. The wind was essential in the final part of threshing. The flat area next to our school was ideal because it was on a high level and caught the wind. A circle was marked out on the hard ground with a stone. It was swept and received about four rows of sheaves. These were placed in a concentric manner, starting from the central spot with heads down, and placed in an ever-increasing circle, until the marked area was reached. I am not certain about any of the dimensions; I was a child at the time and threshing is now undertaken by machine.

The thresher of our 1940s childhood was a rectangular wooden platform, measuring about a metre by three metres, the front bent at an angle. It had big metal rings for attaching the donkey's harness. The under-surface of the platform was punctuated in horizontal lines with shards of flint. The thresher would be turned over on the sheaves at the edge of the circle; the donkey, head in the nosebag munching happily, was led to its post and firmly attached to the waiting platform. The threshing began with an oath from the driver to get his beast moving. To us, it was the only merry-go-round we knew, and we were given the opportunity to sit behind the driver in turn. He would slow the pace so that we would not tip over, but our response was always, "Faster, faster, Barba Nico!" But that speed could not be tolerated for long, as a feeling of giddiness would eventually request a "Stop, oh stop!" until we recovered and asked for more.

Our crop would have been threshed in a day, but more work lay ahead before the wheat became flour and was safely stored in our home. The next stage provided no joy ride for us; nevertheless, we still had the job of bringing sustenance to the workers. The threshed up mass was gathered into a big pile to wait for a strong wind that would eventually sort out the chaff from the grain. As the Earth spun eastward, the sun found its zenith in the vault of the sky. All its shadows then became absolutely vertical. This signalled time for home, lunch and siesta. The afternoon breeze was strong enough to spoil the calm of the sea, enough to make farrows and bring out the sea horses, yet too weak for winnowing. Another day lost; pray for suitable weather for tomorrow!

My childhood is full of memories of asking God to perform miracles that would have solved all our problems. Some of these requests were actually granted, and our faith in the Omnipotent was temporally restored, the way one responds to a rainfall. After we, both young and old, along with our priest in his black robes and colourful pectoral, led a procession out of the village into the stubbly fields and olive groves, it did, in fact, rain the next day. Conversely, there were times when I prayed and prayed for many days for a pair of red shoes, and all God did for me was to let me have them in my dreams. When I looked for them in the morning, I could not find them. Perhaps I had committed a misdemeanour unbeknown to me, of course.

"God, please, may I have a little watch with a red strap?"

He didn't even tantalise me in my dreams. I stopped talking to God after that and fell out with Him. Many years later, when I was fourteen years old, I became a boarder in a Quaker school in Thessaloniki. Miss Vlahou, the Principal, interviewed each girl in her tiny office. She was very kind and gentle with everyone. Once I was ushered into her presence, she said, "Sit down my child."

I sat on the proffered chair and crossed my arms on my lap. In a soft tone and with a little smile she asked, "Do you believe in God?"

My quick response must have astonished her by the look on her face. "Yes, I do believe in Him, but I know He will not drop things in my lap, without efforts on my part."

I had learnt by then that prayer alone wasn't enough to get what I longed for.

Nevertheless, the wind did eventually blow hard enough to

blow away the straw, most of it falling to the ground as a fine dust, which seemed to go in all directions. Every one present was covered in it; it also went into our eyes, ears, nostrils and mouth when we spoke. But that was not all—it invaded our body surfaces and stuck to our sweaty skins. Quite an irritation indeed.

Nico picked up large amounts of the leftover mass in his capacious fork with bent prongs—this was in order to hold a big load—and threw it in air. The wind did the rest. It was amazing to us. We watched a rain of grain falling to the ground and flimsy clouds of chaff flying away in all directions. The residue of chaff and straw was too heavy for winnowing; Nico shovelled it through a big wire sieve. Two to three sacks of glistening golden grain were loaded on Marcos, Uncle Vassili's very obstinate donkey, and taken to our home. Our daily bread was another two steps away before it could be on our table. First the grain had to be washed by hand at the site of the common tap in the wooden trough and dried on the Americana's open concrete rooftop. In due course, it would be taken to the mill and returned to us as flour to be stored safely away from the reach of hungry little mice.

Bread Making

"There are only just two loaves on the shelf, enough for tomorrow," announced our Mother, as if speaking her thoughts out loud. And, that afternoon, Grandma and I went to the countryside to gather wood to fire the bread oven the following morning. Bread was a staple food and had to be prepared.

On my return home, I was sent to fetch a jug full of seawater. We used it as a substitute for salt, which was not then easily obtainable in the village and to enhance the taste of the bread. And that was only the beginning of what was needed. Equipment: one wooden trough, one wire mesh sieve, one scoop, one jug, one bucket, one clean tea-towel, one blanket. Ingredients: six scoops of homegrown wheat-flour yeast, (from the previous week's risen dough), lukewarm water (mixed with the seawater).

Method (my way): Scoop by scoop, I sifted and sieved the flour into the trough. I would grip the sieve with thumbs on its rim and fingers at the base, leaving the palms free to toss the sieve from side to side and separate the flour from the bran. Once this motion was achieved, it had to be maintained. Moving the wrists horizontally with rhythm, the palms hitting the sides of the sieve, making a flap-flap noise, which was very rewarding to my ears. This part of making bread was like a musical game to me.

As the flour passed through the sieve, it formed into a mound in the trough, leaving the bran on the wire mesh. This humble residue provided many benefits. It was used to wipe the food remains from the plates and cutlery prior to washing up and then fed to the poultry. It was also used as a detergent to wash plates, pots and pans. In our home, rinsing under the running tap was a ritual, even though the water had to be fetched from the well or the stand-pipe. It was a ritual that I still observe to this day, and which I tried persistently to introduce to hospital kitchens in my later role as a Clinical Nurse Specialist in infection control. In the 1970s, bran was also in fact elevated to medicinal therapeutic status: out went liquid paraffin, in came bran for the relief/treatment of Irritable Bowel Syndrome, diverticulitis and constipation. Our chickens must have been regularly overdosed, to be sure. The bran was also fed to the snails for twenty-four hours to cleanse their gastrointestinal tract before they were cooked.

The yeast had to be activated the night before. I would make a well in the mound of sifted flour and dig my fingers in the cup containing the cloying, sour smelling yeast, which stuck fast to those hands. It was then eased off with flour and dropped into the floury pit. I would add the warmed liquid, and with both hands, mix the ingredients into dough, shape it into a loaf, sprinkle it generously with flour, place it in the well of the mound and indent it with the sign of the cross. Finally, a clean tea towel and blanket are laid on the trough to maintain and increase the heat generated by the yeast.

The next day, no fewer than three generations of females of the same family participated in this task. In the early Forties, bread was the only sustaining food available to us in the village. Mamma found kneading the dough too strenuous after her asthma attacks. However, after the second rise, when the mixture was light and elastic, she would skilfully shape the dough into loaves of identical size.

Grandma's contribution was to roll up her sleeves, extend the well where the risen yeast was nestling, pour in the warmed liquids and begin mixing the contents turning them into a very sticky mass. Using more of the flour produced a dough ready for kneading again. This next step required speed, a real vigour to maintain the activation of the yeast. If allowed to cool, the yeast bacteria could not multiply and the dough would not rise. Hot liquids have the same effect; they too kill the bacteria.

Hands made into fists, the kneading began.

Dig one hand in, pull it out and dig in the other

The dough becomes elastic; a portion is pulled up, stretched, pulled away from the side and kneaded again until it becomes a smooth and glistening batch, coming halfway up the trough. A handful of flour is dusted on its surface, the cross indented, a clean fresh cloth and blanket placed over the trough and kept away from draughts to rise.

On one particular summer baking day, it fell to me to knead the dough. The reason for this escapes me now; it could have been the time that poor Grandma had dislocated her shoulder. Mamma would have been totally distressed by the event, looking sad and resigned, watching my pitiful attempts to knead the dough.

I moistened my hands in warm water and weighed in, a featherweight with a frame to match, the result of malnutrition and the annual attacks of malaria. It seemed easy at the beginning. However, when the remainder of flour was added to soak up the excess moisture, the volume increased, the dough became a cloying mass like a quagmire. It sucked in my fists and wrists up to the elbows. I tried pulling my hands out of its grip, but the result was tipping me backwards and risking toppling the trough onto myself. It seemed I was hopelessly stuck.

Byron, my little brother, was sent for help. Aunt Kitsa, Mamma's senior, arrived; a big woman was she. She dipped one hand in warm water, held my arm at the elbow and peeled off the dough down to my fingertips, repeating the process with the other arm. "Now go and wash before the dough dries on your skin."

Auntie Kitsa immersed her hands in the warm water, clenched her fists and began to knead with gusto. As one fist went down with a slop-clop sound, the other came up with a sucking noise and a squelch, like donkey's footsteps in clinging mud. The hard work completed, the usual flour dusting, the cross and covers in place, the dough was left to rise for the second time. What must it have been like for our poor Mother looking on so helplessly?

More than one family could be involved in bread making at the same time. Firing the oven required a lot of wood; it made economic sense to invite a neighbour who would fetch another quantity of it along. A pinakoti was put together by Granddad: two parallel planks of wood fixed to a base, intersected with wooden spaces to hold ten ordinary size loaves; a length of linen cloth lined each section, making a nest and sprinkled with flour to receive the anticipated loaf. To avoid confusion over the correct ownership of the end product, one family marked its property by placing two chick peas in the pinakoti. The loaves were placed in the pinakoti by Mamma, who was the expert in shaping all the loaves the same size.

Meanwhile, the oven devoured more wood, and this had to be maintained until the brick floor became white-hot. At this juncture, the residue was raked out of the furnace and dropped to the floor on the side of the oven to be doused with water to prevent a fire after everyone went home. A damp, long-handled mop was used to clean the hot brick floor, and we children were always banned from this area until it was safe to return. Each loaf was placed on an equally long spatula, and lifting the loaf out of its nest in the pinakoti required skill and speed. Mamma excelled in this. She positioned the loaves in the oven in ever-decreasing circles, the oven space being almost taken up completely, allowing only enough room for the pitta. Pitta was the customary batch of dough, stretched to a thickness of two adult fingers in an oval shape, indented by the knuckles of the baker - both the last item to go in and the first to come out.

The oven door was then put in place and secured with a long, heavy pole. The smell of baking in supermarkets, even now, transports me at once to our humble oven shed and transforms me into a child again, awaiting the pitta with other children from the neighbourhood.

The time soon came to check the baking progress. The door would be moved aside; the spatula would enter and out would come the much awaited pitta. The delicious aroma was overwhelming. There was no need to have called us, our olfactory nerves never failed to alert us to the perfectly baked bread. The barely cooled offering would be shared amongst the adults and the children eagerly.

Happy memories...but not entirely so. Carelessness once caused a fire that could have been a tragedy for our family, our neighbours, and probably much of the village if it hadn't been for Pavlos' toothache.

It was a hot summer's night and Pavlos was unable to sleep

because his toothache was continuous. His house could not contain the pain, so he went out into his garden and roamed round and round in agony, but not for long. There in front of him were sparks flying skywards from our oven-shed! It had caught fire even as we slept, which could only have happened if the discarded coals had not been doused sufficiently to put them out.

Forgetting his pain, Pavlos banged repeatedly on our door and on those of our neighbours, who began calling for help and directing operations. Children cried in terror; dogs barked; precious water was thrown in bucketfuls. And, by good fortune, the fire was extinguished. Pavlos returned to his garden, once more nursing his toothache. Sleep and stillness returned, and the night found it had a few more hours to reign uninterrupted after all.

The next morning, however, my siblings and I made a shocking discovery: Our young pullets, perched in the oven shed just inside the door on the left, were still on their perches, but did not move. They were immobile and all an ebony black. The smoke must have killed them as they slumbered, and the flames had charred them. We were very upset, for we had looked on them as pets. But, of course, this was also an economic loss. These birds were food-producers and ultimately, even when no longer laying eggs, found themselves to be much-needed meals on our table.

Still, how much greater a loss it could have been! The fire might have carried off much of our village, after all. We give our thanks to God for Pavlos and that miserable toothache that saved us all.

Our Enemies

As if life weren't hard enough in Ouranoupolis for the Greek exiles from Asia Minor, the families from the land we now know as Turkey had been settled in a remote village, inaccessible to other living souls except by horse, by donkey, or, at worst, by foot. And the war years caused even more poverty, followed by the inevitable infestation by parasites. The soldiers and partisans had their enemy; ours arrived in a different armoury, attacking us, sucking the blood from our childish and sadly malnourished bodies. Some children died, others became ill with secondary infections. Those who recovered eventually looked skeletal and yellow.

We had no defence at all against malarial mosquitoes. We would hear them sometimes, in the quiet of the night, winging into our homes and feeding on us as we slept. At intervals, they would even appear in the daylight hours, when we would set about killing them, usually by squashing them on the whitewashed walls, the white becoming stained with our very own blood. One certain way of killing them was to take aim with a pillow, and this method was clean: no stain on the whitewash.

The bedbugs were indeed a pestilence as well, attacking silently and imperceptibly. They possessed anaesthetic and anticoagulant properties in their mouth parts, so that while we slept, they were able to suck the stuff of life from us. As the anaesthetic gradually wore off, our response was to scratch in our fitful sleep. In the morning, there was often evidence of the injuries—to us and to them—their blood-swollen bodies having been trapped and squashed under our restless limbs. The stains in the bedding revealed the night's battle, and the smell was nauseating.

Lice! A louse is an abominable creature, causing untold misery, embarrassment, and often secondary infections— typhus, for one— and according to my godmother, Joice Loch, I was one of those typhus victims. Staphylococcal infections were another result of the intrepid creatures, as in the case of Irini's, scalp. Head lice and their eggs (nits) are very much in evidence in the daylight hours, moving about between the strands of hair, foraging or cementing their eggs upon them. Their bites and saliva make the lives of their hosts a constant turmoil of scratching and feeling for the offending creatures.

With patience and practice, lice can indeed be trapped. Using the index finger and thumb, the louse is caught. As the two digits come together, holding the parasite firmly to disable it, you must transfer it to the thumbnail and squash the louse to a pulp between them. Looking at my nails now, well-manicured and polished, it is hard to imagine that once they served as such tools of destruction. But back then, my young thumb nails were often stained by blood sucked out of my own scalp.

Fleas are supposed to be shy of light, but are quite daring athletes. I have witnessed amazing leaps that entirely frustrated my attempts to catch and kill them. Their bodies, sideways flattened, are leathery, slipping through finger and thumb and frustrating bids to squash them. Their bites are needle-sharp, causing intense irritation, bleeding and permanent staining of bedding and night-attire.

Revenge on our enemies: How we longed for that! It wasn't the killer-instinct in us. We simply wanted to end the physical suffering inflicted on us by those parasitic armies of insects. There was simply nothing at our disposal then for their elimination. Malarial mosquitoes were ubiquitous—everywhere—and we could not hide from them. Even mosquito nets had not yet reached our village. Help, when it finally came, came from the sky. DDT was sprayed on the stagnant waters, and then the mosquito population was doomed. No more malaria. I was thirteen years old when I suffered the last attack of that illness.

The bedbugs met their end by DDT also, though it was difficult to access their habitat and took a long time to be rid of them. DDT powder was forcefully pumped into every crack visible throughout the home. And for good measure, we also received a dusting from the pump of magic powder. How much did we inhale? What effect did it have on us? Nothing so apparent that I cannot give the highest accolades to that miraculous stuff.

Lice and fleas were not so easy to eliminate. They lived on our bodies and on our clothing. However, a mechanism was devised which gave a lot of satisfaction to the executioner (I speak as one of those satisfied customers), and was effective in producing at least a transitory destruction of the enemy.

This weapon of destruction that I speak of was the heavy hollow iron. The lid had triangular openings to fan the coals in its belly. It was used for pressing clothes. To charge it for battle, the iron had to be filled with a few live coals, then the iron had to be swung from side to side to make all the contents red hot, at which point I would begin to wax lyrical and declare a holocaust against the dastardly insects:

I will find them, all of them,
Wherever they may be,
Lying low and immobile to avoid detection;
I will destroy them all!
The seams of our clothing were like furrows for them and their eggs, which were
glued firmly to the fraying edges. All were in the firing line, however, and
doomed to die.
I will slay them all: not with a sword,
But with fire from Hell,
In the shape of my red-hot weapon!
Their vile bodies will explode;
Blood will splatter, splash, stick to my gun.
The smell will be revolting, abominable...
But this is our blood, the blood of Grandma,
Our parents, my brothers, sisters, even mine,
Swelling their bellies—
They sucked it from our poor, anaemic, malnourished bodies!

Of course, the battle would be lost once more. Their numbers were too great. Our enemies were innumerable. As soon as I put to death one column, another would form in time for the next attack. However, there was a great degree of satisfaction in delivering on threats, swearing to free us from the misery of discomfort. Oh, to be free of the itching and the scratching! What a relief that would be. And to be free of disease...unimaginable!

So, here was my opportunity for revenge, some small measure of satisfaction. The heavy iron, my weapon, was just so heavy in my hands, so hot! But nothing at all would stop me, I vowed. With childish enthusiasm, I launched my attack, and as I record these events after so many years, I still feel a real constriction in my body—I clench my teeth as I write. I am overwhelmed with revulsion, the singeing smell of those incinerated lice and their burning eggs, and the reek of the scorched clothing...

How good it is to be free from infestation.

HAIR WASHING DAY

There was no central heating. There was no hot or even cold water on tap; it had to be drawn from a well. And as the eldest of the three girls, that was a job that was delegated to me. So, I set out, like Jill without Jack, to fetch not one but two pails of water. The well was not up the hill but in a private garden. Grandma obtained permission from the owner.

There came a certain day that we all dreaded: hair washing day. The water-fetching being my duty, I arrived to find the usual dented bucket attached to a wet, coiled rope made from spun goat hair. Then, lowering the bucket into the well, its weight dragged the wet rope between my cold hands, making them sore. The bucket always refused to invert itself in order to fill and I ever lacked the knack of giving it a quick to-and-fro before it hit the water's surface. I couldn't see that far down into the darkness and was afraid of tumbling in with the bucket and rope. To me, it was like looking into a black hole, a chasm, which would pull me screaming into its depth. But eventually, I always managed to fill and bring to the surface that first bucket, spilling cold water on my cold feet, which squelched in the mud around the well's periphery.

Now, I had to hurry and fill the second pail, because both Mamma and Grandma became anxious whenever I was too long returning home. Jerking, tugging and dragging the bucket with renewed enthusiasm and energy simply made my cold fingers and palms even colder, stinging and numb, so that before I knew it, the rope slithered through my hands like a slippery eel, and the full bucket plunged to the bottom of the well. Shock and disappointment mounted, reducing me to tears. I turned round to the path, to go home and alert Grandma, when a few yards ahead of me appeared the owner's mother-in-law like a phantom, a very old,

90

scrawny woman dressed in black pantaloons, wielding a cane at me and shouting, "Out! Out of here! Be gone with you this instant, you thieving urchin! Go now, go! And find a way of getting that bucket up!"

She shrieked in such a shrill voice that I was terrified of her and fled the garden at once to escape the wrath of the old crone. Surely I wasn't the first person to have had the misfortune of losing hold of the bucket. After all, I was only a child! I was also baffled as to how she could expect me to both flee and get the bucket up at the same time.

I arrived home in tears, no broken crown like poor Jack, just a broken little heart. Grandma soothed me and wiped away my tears, and then she and I pulled the tripod from our hearth, the one we used for the cooking pot. We attached the usual goat-hair rope to it and repaired once again to the evil garden. No sign of my pursuer. Under Grandma's supervision, I lowered the tripod into the well. I allowed it to reach the bottom, then tossed it and jerked it to and fro innumerable times until—at last!—I hooked the submerged bucket and brought it triumphantly to the surface.

"Well done, my child. Bravo!" exclaimed Grandma. And we went home with smiles.

Now, hair washing was an ordeal for our mother and for all the siblings, but most especially for the three of us girls. It was a lengthy and painful procedure. Making a lather with the rough homemade soap was a tear-jerking assault upon our scalps. Combing the strands of the tangled hair and removing as many lice and cemented nits as was possible—the latter, by Mamma's thumb and finger-nails—was protracted torture. Many years later, when I saw monkeys for the first time, I was amazed at their dexterity in using more or less the same method to delouse one another.

Who would be first? No answer.

"The eldest goes first!" chorused my younger sisters.

Reluctantly, I bent my head and submitted to what felt like a torrent of water drenching my head, followed by Mamma's firm hand applying the hard bar of soap over my hair, making painful circular movements, trying to create lather.

91

The fine-tooth comb was another tool of torture, although, of course, a necessary evil. Mamma was very sympathetic and apologetic for having to use it on our tangled tresses, but it was the only means available for disentangling hair and removing at least some of the infestation. Rinsing the hair was like drowning in hot muddy water. I looked up with red eyes and tears, a sorry sight indeed.

We dried our hair by the fireside, elbowing each other and arguing about priority, edging always to sit closer to the hearth, until a gust of wind down our incontinent chimney belched black smoke that enveloped us, making our eyes smart again and forcing us to scuttle away like distressed mice. The smoke would bring on a coughing fit for Mamma, resulting in an asthma attack. This sobered us up. We returned to the hearth, tossing our heads this way and that to dry our wet hair.

Science, I believe, has produced a battery-operated fine-tooth comb, which electrocutes lice and nits as the hair is combed. What a miraculous invention indeed! If only we had one when my sisters and I were children. That, and hairdryers. Those two items would have saved countless hours of pain and waiting for three young children who seldom knew how to sit still.

Village Medicine

As I stated previously, my mother's skills as village nurse were much sought after. One of her methods was the use of Cupping (Ventouses), simple or with cuts—a treatment appropriate for persons who were suffering from a congestive chest cold. Both young and old were subjected to the procedure with successful outcomes. I still have a vivid vision of Mamma in the bedroom we shared with Grandma. One of my siblings was the patient awaiting the cupping, and with understandable trepidation.

Mamma stood on the left by a shelf. On it was her equipment, comprising a fork, cotton wool, a reel with sewing thread, a small glass, a box of matches and a bottle of blue liquid. She picked up the fork, wound the wad of cotton-wool round the prongs, securing it with a piece of thread. She opened the bottle containing the blue liquid—methylated spirit. She poured some into the small glass and plunged the fork in it, head first.

Her attention moved on to the patient, a reassuring chat in progress. The little patient rolled over, the thin back exposed and the bedding turned down. Mamma removed the intoxicated fork from its alcoholic soak, struck a match and set the wad alight, making it look like a flaming torch. With her right hand, she picked up a cup (ventouse), inserted the flaming torch into it to create a vacuum, and placed it adroitly on the patient's back. Three more cups are applied strategically to make a square. Four little fleshy domes inside the glass cups—they look like cloches used to protect delicate plants.

The patient whimpers, begging Mamma to remove them. They are left in place only for a few minutes, but to the patient, it seems a very long time. A special technique is then applied to prevent pain when removing the cups. Mamma would press gently with her index finger of the left hand near the rim of the cup; with her right hand, she would ease it off by disrupting the vacuum. It would come away painlessly, making a plopping sound, much to the relief of the patient. Then, she followed up with a light massage using a little methylated spirit. Our patient turned over and settled down into a foetal position, Mamma bending down to him, whispering. There is tenderness and love: all is well–sleep will soon take over.

The cut version of ventouses, however, is more like a minor surgical intervention because it involves small lacerations. I myself have been a recipient on more than one occasion, though it is undertaken only in cases of severe respiratory congestion, when coughing and fever are present but fail to respond to the simple cupping or other homemade potions.

The skin is cleansed with methylated spirit again; a fold of flesh is pinched between the thumb and the index finger of one hand, and a razor blade is firmly held by the thumb and index finger by the dominant hand. This is the moment, of course, when the patient fears the onset of pain, but Mamma was always a skilled operator: her touch was always light as she nicked the skin in four places within the periphery of the anticipated cups. The process is repeated at speed four times: Mamma lights the charged fork, creates the vacuum and places the cups over the lacerated skin. The flesh under the glass rises into little domes, dark red blood oozing in glistening blobs, looking rather like blackcurrant berries. The viscous liquid collects inside the rim of the cups, looking like a thick red rubber band, and this is the signal to remove the cups.

Mamma carefully manoeuvred the removal without blood spills, wiping the cut skin lightly with a swab dipped in the methylated spirit to prevent microbes entering the cuts and causing infection. This would make young patients scream aloud: "No more, Mamma, stop now, please!" Adults must have bitten hard on their bedding to prevent their own shrieks. I must add that, although I underwent the above procedure more than once, my back is not scarred. Mamma's touch was certainly very light. And her touch and her skills were renowned throughout the village.

Many knew the story of our neighbour, for instance. Sotiris, our neighbour, was shipwrecked in his small rowing boat during a freak storm. Soaked to the skin and exposed to the elements for many hours before being rescued, he became very ill with a high fever. Martha his wife, nursed him as best as she knew how in their little lean-to barn, heated by just the usual small fire in one corner. But she nursed him there in order to keep the family home like a doll's house; for Martha, was house-proud. She had broderie Anglaise on every window in the house. It was said that she even kept a plant in the grate. The front steps leading up to her door were a dazzling white, and on either side of them was a profusion of plants. I remember asking her for wallflowers at Easter time.

The patient in the barn simply failed to get better, however, and our mother was called over the garden hedge, for there were no fences or stone walls anywhere in the village. It took a lot of persuading on Mamma's part to get Sotiris transferred into the house and to light a fire in the virgin grate before the cupping could be undertaken. But it must have been comforting indeed for the patient to have so much attention and care, and in a warm room, to enjoy a massage after the cupping and to settle down to a much-needed sleep.

Mamma advised Martha that it was necessary to give the patient plenty of mountain tea and to sacrifice a chicken to make him soup. "Feed him well," she said, "to help his recovery, and in a few weeks' time, he may be well enough to return to living and sleeping in the barn." Which was exactly what happened.

It wasn't only husbands who were brought thus to our mother. Young mothers brought their colicky infants to our house to receive Mamma's attention. She would place the baby over her lap on its tummy, expose the tiny pink back and proceed to massage very gently, starting at the nape of its head and bringing her oiled hands to the sides of the chest. The baby eventually stopped crying and went to sleep. Was it the massage or our mother's way of handling and comforting those in discomfort or pain? I suspect that both contributed to the relief of the problem.

Some problems were trickier. Anna, our friend, had a wound in the palm of her hand. It was a sinus—a little tunnel in the muscle under the skin that failed to heal, so she came to ask our mother for help. It was the first time I witnessed this cure.

Mamma, using her knitting needle, I have no idea how she sterilised it, gently inserted a thin strip of clean bed linen it into the wound to act as a wick to drain it. Anna came every day for a change of dressing. I remember it was smelly and looked very yellow. Mamma redressed the wound in the same way as before and continued the treatment until the wick came out at last wet but not soiled.

Anna's palm healed completely.

And so did Yianna's impetigo.

Yianna had long blond hair that had become extremely matted as a result of an attack upon her scalp by microbes, causing the infection called impetigo. Her mother brought her to our house for our mother's inspection and a possible cure. Again, I can vividly recall the scene. It was a bright sunny day; Mamma was sitting on a step outside the lean-to, Yianna on the step below, between her knees. My mother was armed with scissors: the blond tresses were soon landing on the ground. Yianna was crying, shedding bitter tears at the loss of her hair and at enduring such pain, yet all her mother kept telling her was, "skasse, skasse" "Shut up, shut up!"

It must have been an excruciating experience for the poor child because much of the hair was stuck to her scalp. Mamma, as I remember, worked very fast. She made a cream with the sulphur powder used by my Grandma to dust the vines, plus some other ingredient, lost to memory. This she applied all over the prepared area of the poor girl's head and covered it with a headscarf. The treatment worked, and the infection disappeared. Best of all, Irini's blond hair grew back once again.

Many years later, on a visit to the village, I asked to see Yianna, though her grandson told me it would be a waste of my time. "She can't see or hear. She sleeps all the time, sitting on that chair there in the corner."

I found her dosing, sure enough. Kneeling beside her, I spoke her name, at which she opened her dull and clouded eyes and peered at me for a few seconds. Recognition dawned: She knew me by my voice. "It is you," she exclaimed with much surprised pleasure, uttering my name.

"Yianna, do you remember the day my mother cut off all your lovely hair?"

She smiled at me. "Oh, yes, how can I forget? It was very painful, but your good mother made me better, God rest her soul. Praise God! She was so kind and gentle."

Of course, there were others too, so many others, who were grateful for the nursing that my mother provided.

A tall man, one of the very few in my world, arrived at our house in distress one day, dental decay having no respect for height. He was clasping the side of his face and asking Mamma to make him better. It took a long time to boil water over a wood fire. Mamma poured the hot water into a bowl, dropped the yellow poppy seeds in it, and placed it in front of the seated patient. He bent his covered head and then opened his cavernous mouth over it. I squatted on the floor for a better view and looked up to see him, dribbling into the bowl.

Eventually, he raised his head and announced that his toothache had left him. Looking down at the bowl, he saw the poppy seeds floating on the surface of the inhalation and exclaimed triumphantly, "There!" The offending microbes had been killed, he believed: they had fallen into the water—he could see them quite plainly! Mamma did not correct him, and he went home with a smile on his rosy face.

Not that my mother could handle all medical matters.

I remember a man called Mr. Petridis. He was short and stocky, his complexion was sallow, his hair was tightly curled, he wore spectacles half way down his nose, and his hands were dirty with oil and grease. He repaired watches and sewing machines, extracted teeth and gave injections. Mamma took me along to visit him one afternoon, and as soon as we arrived, they began an earnest conversation in Turkish. Whenever grown-ups didn't want us to know what they were discussing, they spoke together in Turkish,

Mr. Petridis as I later learned was a refugee from Caesarea. His mother tongue was Turkish; mamma, having lived in Turkey as a child spoke that language fluently. The outcome of the consultation was a quinine injection for me. There was no warning; a needle was forcefully thrust in my buttock! It was a most excruciating pain and a humiliating experience. The needle must have been blunt and the liquid probably quinine. I came home in tears. It hurt all day, but there is no record of complications.

In 2007, I was told by an older woman a dental treatment she had witnessed being carried out by Mr. Petridis. A sufferer of toothache had gone to have his tooth extracted but felt very nervous. To reassure him, Mr. Petridis stepped out into his yard, went up to his donkey, opened the unsuspecting beast's mouth plunged his hand straight in with pliers and brought forth a giant tooth.

"Look—not a problem! Open your mouth," he commanded.

"Did he?" was my question.

Yes, for he had no choice but to allow himself to be tortured. And what about the poor beast? It had no choice either. But, did it not kick, bray, resist? Evidently not so much as the patient.

All medical matters have hugely improved, but in the days of my childhood, there were simply no medicines to relieve pain and coughs, nor creams to apply to sores. Our mother made use of anything she could find that nature provided: the silky inner dry leaves of onions were ideal for covering wounds and sores, while more succulent leaves were applied on boils, to encourage them to come to a head. A really persistent cough was treated with a disgusting, foul-smelling concoction of crushed garlic in equally unpalatable liquid, camphor.

Seasickness was relieved with a teaspoon of sugar and pulverised coffee, and in that case, it was actually worth feeling sick, just to get such a delicious treatment. Constipation was not very common since our diet lacked substance and consisted of too many horta (wild edible greens) for that. When a suppository was required, however, Mamma made one from a sliver of homemade soap. She smoothed it and rolled it into a cylinder with one end a little pointed, moistened it in warm water and inserted it gently. It was effective; the only side effect I recollect was discomfort and stinging. Perhaps the homemade soap had too much caustic soda for internal use.

Our enterprising mother decided to have a go at making luxury soap. I remember a shallow wooden box, like those used as seed trays, with pink soap in it, cut in diamond shapes. What I do not recollect is using any of it. I supposed it was for the adults only.

The soap we used every day for hygiene and for the laundry was earth coloured, a by-product of olive oil. It looked like dried-up soil and felt rough. It didn't slide through our fingers like today's soap. And it was certainly a tear-jerker when used for hair washing.

Many paths to cleanliness and health were painful in those days.

This home remedy was not our mother's and should surely have been banned. It was carried out, I recall, on our youngest brother, only a toddler at the time and suffering from a sore throat. Smaro, the self-appointed specialist, decided to treat it. She sat by the hearth, spat on her big thumb and pressed it in the cool ash. The patient's mouth was held wide open and his little body restrained, while Smaro's thumb dived in and held down the tonsils. The distress and retching of the child are difficult to describe but can be easily imagined. It was a cruel and even dangerous procedure. Did our mother know what was about to happen? Was she present, or too ill and out of breath to protest and prevent it? I can no longer remember.

Even worse, though, was the cure produced by roasting in the bread oven—one to frighten even the bravest. It was a holocaust: It looked as if the patient was about to be roasted alive, his death sealed. The oven was inside a stable, opposite the garden of our paternal grandparents. As children, we associated it with Christmas, because a cow lived inside.

The oven cure was for a man who had been stung by a scorpion. The entire village population of children (barefoot urchins, I was one of them), thronged to watch the murder by roasting of Barba Mihali. (Older men were referred to as Barba, meaning Uncle, and women as Thea, meaning Aunty; we believed that in a real sense we were all from one family).

Barba Mihali was brought to the stable on a ladder padded with a tserya: a thick woollen rug used by shepherds when sleeping on the hard ground, half of it under the body, the other half over it during the cold of the winter. The oven was already fired and slightly cooled down. He was shoved into its depth like the Easter lamb and the door closed after him!

The waiting seemed interminable. Silent fear gripped everyone. I cannot remember for how long poor Barba Mihali was baked in there, but someone opened the oven and spoke with the patient, so he was still alive then. How much longer will it be, I asked myself, before he is brought back out of the furnace, dead or alive? We were impatient to find out.

The reason for the hot oven was to make the patient perspire quickly and profusely, so that the poison from the sting would be eliminated from his system. At least on this occasion, it was a most successful outcome. Barba Mihali continued to work in his fields, had several more children, and lived to a ripe old age. Indeed, though I was but a child at the time of the scorpion incident, Mihali was still alive and working when I had children of my own. On our visits to the village, he gave my little daughters rides on his docile and ancient donkey.

THE KING (AN ELEGANT FOWL)

His yellow feet were bound together and hooked onto a nail on a tree branch. The headless body swung forlornly in the early morning breeze. Gravity pulled his wings earthwards, half extended. The long and beautiful feathers spread out like fingers, and blood dripped from the ruggedly severed neck, dripping in order to ensure white meat for dinner. His blood made irregular purple patches on the dry soil below him. The proud head, eyes wide open and glazed, stared unseeing now into infinity, the powerful and punishing beak open, and the pink tongue protruding visibly. The proud royal head lay abandoned on the ground, where his executioner had tossed it. Well done, Macduff!

Would anyone mourn his ignominious end? Those who suffered great physical pain under his dominance were bound to be relieved at his passing. Cousin Katherine would again threaten him, without doubt, for his viciousness. His mighty beak had all too often drawn blood from her Achilles' tendon. Here was gratitude from loyalty: he bit the hand that fed him, though in this case, it was the foot he attacked.

He and his fellow creatures enjoyed a free life in open country; their diet was always plentiful and further enriched with the corn they fed them. Chuckling to themselves and scratching the soil for tasty morsels of worms, seeds, and drops of abandoned fruit, his hens lay under the cool shade of trees, to sleep and to dream of a life without the King. This was their daily routine, regardless of his non-presence. Except for the egg-layers—they firmly sat on their nests, laid an egg, and sang long and loud for all in the universe to hear: ko-o ko-koh ko-oko-o, koh koko oko, ko kokoko, ko, on and on...

The King had been tall and solidly built. He looked magnificently resplendent in his richly colourful plumage. His head was adorned with exquisitely fine feathers, which shone iridescent in sunlight. His thick red comb was topped with a lacy edge like a crescent crown, running from his forehead towards his back. His wattles were just as crimson, and as he strutted along, those magnificent appendages would swing tremulously and seductively from side to side. His bright amber eyes sparkled, darting in all directions, seeking pleasure and fending off his young rivals. He always moved with purpose, confidence and authority. He would lift one yellow leg with a spur at the back, and with the curled talons of the foot, grip the patch of dry earth underneath him, as if he were about to hold up the globe. He would repeat the action with his other leg, then would stand still and tall, raising that regal head high, extending his wings, flapping them—once, twice—to announce to his kingdom that he was the Lord of all the creatures around him with a trumpeting: cock-a-doodle-do, cock-a-doodle-do!

Looking about him, his roving eye would catch sight of a happy hen: busy looking for a little beakful to pass the time and exercise her digestion, quite unaware of her entirely hedonistic, libidinous and testosterone-fuelled master hurtling towards her. He would land on top of her, pin her hard to the ground, then keep her from escaping by pecking at her comb and gripping her sides with those powerful claw-like talons. She would struggle and screech to no avail; he was very strong—merciless—and always had his way. Feeling victorious, he would again flap his wings and regale the company with a tuneful cock-a-doodle-do, cock-a-doodle-do—declaring, 'Look at me all of you—especially you—the young pretenders on the periphery! I am the King!'

Despite his narcissism, his generosity was not reserved for self-pleasure and procreation only. He was the caring patriarch of his flock. He would look for food, scratching vigorously at the parched earth, and as soon as he was successful, he would call, of course, only the hens, with a kok-kok-kokok. They would answer the call and arrive to receive his gift—the pain forgotten and all forgiven.

The young cockerels could watch from a distance. Their only chance to steal a few beakfuls was when the master's attention was distracted by yet another hen and he ran after her. They jumped at the chance as quickly as the King jumped on the hen. As for the young pretenders, only one of them would be spared the knife—the rest were destined for the pot when they grew fat enough to make a good meal. The one lucky cockerel that remained would one day succeed him, unless he abused his power and attacked cousin Katherine. Then beware, young prince! Power corrupts. Your wretched life will be on the line, at the mercy of George's knife, and your end will be the beginning for another, now waiting in the wings to wear your crown.

When the sun began to leave the land in darkness, the King led his flock to the coup. The hens jumped up on the perches, and jostling for position, they would peck at a neighbour on the right or on the left and talk about the day's events. With a chorus of korr-korr-korr, they would bury their heads in silky-soft breast feathers or tuck their head under a plump wing. In his turn, the master murmured a few fowl words with a korkorkor-kok-kok, in a most soporific voice, almost like a blessing. Finally, order and silence were restored. They all would settle down for the night, and let sleep transport them to a more peaceful kingdom.

George had entered the sleeping-quarters that day under cover of darkness, and with the aid of a torch, soon found the King sleeping peacefully away. Unbeknown to the King, his nemesis had arrived. The end was nigh. George put his hands over the slumbering creature, picked him up and carried him out of the coup. The King continued to dream his fowl rooster dreams while he was being transferred to the yard and placed in an upturned wooden box. The box was placed well away from the coup to await daylight.

Before the sun returned to Earth to light up the day and awaken the sleeping world, George was ready with his sharpened knife. He grasped the cockerel by the legs and wings. The hapless creature quickly awoke, and realizing the danger, he resisted and struggled against the unprovoked attack. George was the more powerful, however. There was no escape; especially as the King's assailant placed the yellow feet under the weight of his right foot and the powerful wings under the left foot, to immobilize him. The helpless body shook and trembled spasmodically, pecking defiantly at George's right foot. George then picked up the angry, terrified head with his left hand and pulled it up towards him to stretch the neck. He placed the knife on the King's throat and pulled it across swiftly. Blood spurted in all directions. Body and head came apart with a thump and a click. The body began to convulse in its death-throes, surrendering to its fate.

George tossed the head to the ground.

There was something out of character in the coup that morning, when daylight forced all those bleary amber eyes to open. The King, who routinely brought them to consciousness with a twittering of kok, kok, kok kok, was missing. Where had the master gone? One audacious cockerel flapped his wings a couple of times, lifted his young head high and stretching his neck, let out a juvenile cock-a-doodle-do, cock-a-doodle-do in a hoarse and croaky voice:

"The King is dead! Long live the King!"

A not-so-bloodless coup, but there were no dissidents to the change in power.

When Katherine opened the coup in the morning and as usual, the hens poured out like lemmings, shoving and pushing, like children anxious to leave the classroom and enjoy a break. They scattered across the ground under the olive and fig trees and over the fields to live another day with a new king.

But what followed for their master was nothing short of mutilation and humiliation. The water in the caldron had just come off the boil. The decapitated fowl was held by its scaly yellow feet, plunged into the water and held submerged for several minutes. This was to ease the removal of feathers without damaging the flesh. Nothing was spared; even the head was subsequently dropped into the caldron, as very little of the bird was ever wasted. Thrown on the chopping board unceremoniously, the once-beautiful bird had become unrecognizable; the clumped and matted feathers stuck together and had lost their lustre. I remember how Katherine and George plucked with care to reveal a stark, white body, nude and inglorious. All beauty had gone.

See as the fowl is turned on his back; George's knife slices him open from the soft part just below the breastbone to the end of the body. Katherine inserts her hand in the cavity and removes the entrails. The crop is discarded together with the smelly intestines. What remain are the heart and liver, without the gallbladder and the gizzard, which are chopped up and added to the stuffing or soups. The head is also plucked and cooked. The mother of the house is usually the person who will eat it. It was so in the old days when food was in short supply: Mothers gave the best to the father and the children and kept the less attractive parts for themselves.

How the great diminish as they age! The King was an old rooster and therefore his flesh was very tough, and even after prolonged boiling, was only fit for avgolemono (lemon soup). Still, there were worse fates than being decapitated...

THE COCKEREL WHO DARED

In 1980, so I am told, decades after I had left our village, a cockerel met his end in a most tragic manner. He had been the dominant male in the neighbourhood for a long, long time in chicken years and took advantage of his age, position and power to enjoy a life of hedonism. He terrorized the other fowls into submission, both cocks and hens, and even became aggressive towards humans. Small children often became a target for his terror attacks. It was just such an incident that brought about his horrifying end.

A little girl of five years was playing in the road outside her home, when suddenly; she was furiously attacked by an angry cockerel. She squatted on the spot and buried her head in her lap, screaming for help. Undeterred, he pecked at her head, fast and viciously, until her father responded to her distressed call and drove the attacker away.

The next day, the child's father called on his neighbour, offering to exchange a young cockerel for that aged but still virile bird that had attacked his daughter. Did the old cockerel's owner ask himself the reason for such a generous request? Had he known, would he have granted it? The story surely tells of his indifference. He had acquired a young cockerel, after all, that would service all of his hens for a long time. Why should he bother to concern himself with the logic of such a peculiar exchange?

The relieved and grateful recipient went home with his prize, and the cockerel's heart beat nervously under its wings. He seemed to know with his little cockerel brain that vengeance was lurking around the corner. The aggrieved, avenging parent took himself to the shade of his balcony by the water-tap and began his revenge.

A strong bird is difficult to handle anyway, but an anxious one becomes unmanageable indeed. In this case, I am told, it became a real fight, with claws, beak, and wings. Tugging and pulling this way and that, the man soon had the upper hand and began the punishment with alacrity. He plucked the bird naked—and fully alive, I might add—his beautiful wing feathers were pulled off one-by-one, scattered around him, the small and downy feathers flying away in clouds over the garden. At last, released from the clutches of his tormentor, bleeding, humiliated and stumbling away, the cockerel looked like a dead chicken somehow escaping from the butcher's premises.

"Look, everyone! What on earth is that phantom running in the yard?" cried an old hen.

They stood still, hens and cockerels alike, and then without prompting, they all gave chase. They caught up with the unfortunate creature, brought him down and began to attack his bare and bleeding body, tearing at his flesh. He was lynched by the mob...by his peers...by his kindred. Did they have a score to settle? It is probable. The younger resented and feared him; the hens were terrified by his abrupt and rough mounting (though it is also equally possible that they took him for an alien, as they had never seen anything quite like him before).

Man had his revenge and wiped the slate clean that day, but what a sad example of inhumanity that man can be so vengeful towards his fellow creatures.

To Kill a Cockerel

Our Grandmother was in great pain; her shoulder blade broken in a fall. I remember her sitting on a chair in the kitchen. A man, not a doctor (none existed in our village), used one of the baby's wrappers as a sling for her arm and placed a cloth soaked in beaten egg white to make it stick on her back and prevent movement of the broken bones. Poor Grandma I can still see her even now, looking helpless and letting little groans of pain escape between her lips. Grandma was now out of action. Mamma would be able to carry on with everything as long as she was free from her asthma, but when an attack gripped her, it paralyzed her for hours or days.

That was why I had to volunteer, to act the grown-up and behead the insidious fowl.

The pullet to be made into soup would always be a surplus male; hens were for producing eggs, after all. They were only used for the pot when old and unproductive. This time, the lot fell on a very young male: He was jet black (probably one of Mavroula's sons) with a yellow beak and feet. I chased the hapless victim round the garden many times. He was faster than me. He also took off on short flights to frustrate me.

His undoing was to try escaping through the hedge. But I captured this immature cockerel, distraught and terrified, by cornering him against the thick bushes. It was difficult to carry him. He shivered and struggled to free himself and became all beak, legs and claws but I was determined to do my duty. Mamma, sitting in her usual place in the lean-to under the shade of the sprawling vine overhead, watched the chase and its effect on both bird and child.

"Let him go, my child. He may be young, but he is too strong for you to kill."

"I can do it—see if I don't!" The challenge was noted and accepted.

Of course, I had witnessed the procedure innumerable times, but I hadn't reckoned on the emotional effect it would evoke in me. I was still only a child, full of childish aspirations to emulate the acts of adults. Mamma had a pained and resigned look on her sad face. Her breathing made her chest rise and fall as if the air were being forced out of her.

I was in a highly emotional state, full of bravado. I held my quarry by one hand firmly against my body. I proceeded by placing the wriggling legs under my right foot, leaning heavily with all my light weight, as I had seen adults do many times. I folded his wings, secured them under my left foot and regained my balance. His head in the meantime, with eyes darting in all directions, was thrusting about, attempting to pull away from its captor, but I held firm. With my right hand, I picked up the small black vegetable knife and reached with the left hand for the doomed head. The yellow beak opened and closed in vain, attempting to peck at my hand. I grasped the head and stretched it as hard as I could to straighten it so that the feathers would not prevent the knife reaching the flesh. I had no idea at that moment where or how to start. My helpless mother simply looked on with pleading eyes that told me to leave it alone.

The scene was set: the cockerel's body between my feet struggling to regain his freedom, and I, the child executioner, trembling all over from excitement and sudden, overwhelming fear. The knife made no impact on the outstretched neck of my too young cockerel; I was using it like a saw. I began to panic and feared I would fail to reach the skin...

Success and failure arrived simultaneously! I cut the skin. Blood spurted. I let go. Screaming and terrified, I fell into Mamma's protective arms crying "Imarton!" (Forgive me!) between my sobs. The traumatized but still living cockerel disappeared into the garden to grow and serve the chickens to his best virile capacity. As far as I remember, he never again made it on the list as a candidate for soup.

HUNGER

In those days, three girls could barely suppress our hunger. We hunted the starving birds and lured them to their deaths. When the snow blanketed our earth, we dashed into the garden in flimsy footwear, treading on the virgin snow, shivering, and breathing in the chilled air. We made our way under the skeleton of the almond tree, here using our bare hands to clear an area the size of the flour sieve. We would set the sieve there, with a stick at a right angles attach a string to it and lead the string back to and through the kitchen window. We then ran back to the kitchen, warmed our chilled limbs by the hearth, knelt on the seat, and pressed our faces against the cold glass windowpane to watch our bird trap.

The soil under it looked dark, so full of promising grubs, and soon, as hoped, a black bird arrived. We pulled the string, but the bird was too fast for us and easily escaped. We spent many hours watching and wishing with famished anticipation. More birds came and began pecking their brothers and sisters out of the way, to be the first to scratch the earth and find its fruit, unaware that they were putting their little heads in the noose.

In time, we caught a few feathered creatures. When we picked up the little birds in our hands—they were trembling from fear just as we were—but hunger has no time for sentimentality or guilt. We tore off their tiny heads and roasted them on the hot embers. The smell of burning feathers and flesh was nauseating, yet appetising. We dismembered their bodies and shared them between the three of us, but there was little of substance; just a taste of flesh. When my children and grandchildren read this monstrous account, they will be horrified and call me 'a fowl murderer.' Now I encourage birds to my garden and feed them, to help them survive, so that their Maker may forgive and absolve me of my past behaviour.

Olive Picking

Olive picking was a task for all able family members, young and old. Anyone who could pick up even a small stone the size of a marble was capable of joining the olive harvest. But I remember very few occasions when our father came along with us. On one of those rare occasions, one of my younger sisters, Angeliki, and I went to pick olives with him. The olive grove was in Servikon, on the north side of the village, on the other side of the peninsula, at least 3 kilometres from home. It is now a tourist attraction for the more discerning; the sea is less crowded and the beach is sandy, the road has been made accessible for farm implements and cars. This year, one of my daughters and her family went there by car. I would never have imagined in my childhood that one day transport would be available by means other than carts drawn by oxen, donkeys, mules and some horses. I had yet to find out what a machine on wheels looked like.

Our route, shared by other traffic—carts and animals—was a narrow path, twisting and uneven but downhill all the way to our destination. We walked barefoot, even at that time of year for olives are harvested in October to November, so we must have felt the chill. Where were the galoshes that Grandfather Yiannis had made for our feet?

We brought our food along with us. Mamma had provided a small enamelled bowl with a handful of dry, pickled black olives, to which she had added half a loaf of heavy black bread, an onion, a bottle half full with olive oil and vinegar, all tied together in a tea towel, which must have looked like the one Dick Whittington carried to London. The water was in a pitcher. It had a pinecone for a stopper, and our father was in charge of it.

111

It was cold and back-aching work. The ground under the olive trees was rough and strewn with thorns from the prickly shrubs nearby. Our chilled fingers often came in contact with them and were made very sore by the thorns. Under the holly-like shrubs grew wild cyclamens. They were miniatures with exquisite fairy-like heads. Some of them were white and some fuchsia pink.

Time to eat. We untied the tea towel. Father placed the onion on its head atop a stone. He raised his iron fist and brought it down, flattening the upstanding king of fine cuisine so that it suddenly looked like a flower, its virgin white layers exposed like soiled flower petals that had been trodden under foot. Then, like Jesus, he broke the half loaf of bread and passed it round. He gave a vigorous shake to the bottle containing the olive oil and vinegar, poured it over the pickled olives, and made us eat. We dipped our bread in the bowl and picked the olives with our fingers, relishing our well-deserved meal. Oh, it did taste good, but it made us very thirsty indeed, as a copious amount of salt is used to preserve olives. We filled big sacks with olives and left them to be brought to the village by animal transport. We also filled little sacks, slung them on our childish backs and took the long, rough and tortuous road to the village with father ahead of us, striding along with giant steps, impossible to keep up with.

A change in the weather for the worse made our return home treacherous. The sky looked overcast, angry and streaked with lightening. Resounding bouts of thunder frightened us. The storm was further heralded by huge raindrops. We tried vainly to reassure each other, but our father snapped back at us. "Walk faster and don't talk! There is nothing to fear. We will soon be home." Heavy, cold rain began to beat down upon us. It ran like a stream under our feet, turning our path in to a mud bath. Walking barefoot, soaked to the skin, we shivered from the bitter cold, exposure and exhaustion. We arrived home at last, dispirited and tearful, to find our mother distraught with anxiety about us. Such was harvesting with our father!

Gathering olives with our grandmother, as we usually did, was quite a different experience, although that, too, could be an adventure. I disliked climbing trees then for fear of falling to the ground below. "Climb up and shake the top branches, paedi mou (my child)!"

"But Grandma," I would say, "I am afraid of falling."

"You will be alright. Just keep repeating: Mother of God, Jesus Christ, the Holy Saints and St. John."

I climbed up the little tree, repeating the mantra, and began to move slowly, shaking the small branches. Suddenly, the branch upon which I was standing began to creak and break.

"Grandma," I cried, "I am falling! Please help me!" The branch broke but I had landed on one exactly beneath it.

"There you are. I told you the little prayer would save you!"

My faith in her was absolute, I believed her of course and never doubted again.

Nature's Bounty

Wild mushrooms were just as tasty as any meal and more often part of our diet than meat. They grew on the bark of pine trees, and our mother was an expert at recognising the non-poisonous species. She was always confident in what she'd collected and prepared many an appetising meal for the family. On one occasion, however, Mamma was mistaken. She had actually gathered a poisonous one. She must have had doubts not to serve it to us, but instead ate only some of it herself. She was soon extremely ill with vomiting and shock. Poor Grandma called for help and of course there was no doctor. A visiting ship's captain came to the rescue, luckily. I cannot explain the treatment that saved our mother but I do remember the captain's advice concerning the safe way of eating wild mushrooms: During the cooking, always put a silver spoon in the pot, and if the spoon becomes tarnished, there is poison. Mushrooms were not the only wild gifts we gathered. There were no greens like cabbage, broccoli or sprouts in the Winter season. But when the Spring brought welcome rain and made the earth fertile, many edible green plants began to show themselves along the hedgerows. Mothers and young girls, armed with deep wicker baskets and worn-out knives, left the village together to gather horta (wild greens), happy to be in the countryside. It was an opportunity for the young children to explore and look for bird nests and for the older girls and women to gossip and to sing. Only women and children went on these expeditions, for such trips were beneath male dignity in the winter.

It was also a competition: Who would collect the most horta? Whose will be the first basket to be filled? The grown-ups began in earnest, their knives thrust into the yielding earth, eager hands grasping the plants. Speed was essential, no chatting now. Each tender plant had its root removed as it was lifted. Handfuls of greens were thrown hurriedly into the gaping baskets until they simply could contain no more. This year, 2008, visiting my village produced a nostalgia for the horta harvest and propelled me to one of the gathering parts of the countryside. I went along with a younger friend, armed with a wicker basket and a kitchen knife. We gathered horta and recorded the event with a digital camera. This time, I didn't have to wait for my turn in the cold at the standpipe: I prepared the horta in my own kitchen.

Returning home like an army of ants, we collected buckets and made for the standpipe. There was one to be found in each small square throughout our village, shared by a number of dwellings. We began to wash the greens; it was a long and laborious chore. We queued for the water for hours, as the day began to depart and the early evening took its place. We felt the chill of the spring air, and our cheerful mood left us. Impatience hovered over us. Such days ware long days for the adults but even longer for us children.

My turn arrived to fill up with water. It was very cold, sending shudders up my spine. I plucked handfuls of greens from the basket and plunged them in, pressing them down and shaking them. It took more than one wash to rinse out the soil, especially as some of the plants had curly leaves.

A basketful of greens is reduced, after boiling, to a quarter of its size. Nevertheless, it made a welcome meal, especially by adding a little drizzle of olive oil and a squeeze of lemon, when available; rather more often it was homemade vinegar. The greens were eaten with black pickled olives and homemade bread, heavy and often stale, but edible. It certainly satiated our hunger. Mushrooms and greens weren't the only gifts mamma would cull from the natural world. How about snails for lunch?

After the rain came the sun, and with the sun came the snails. We hastened along the hedges, harvesting them, and when we had filled the bucket, we returned home, handing our quarry to the adults for another meal. Such a blessing from nature!

Preparation of the snails before cooking was essential in order to produce a palatable meal. I remember my paternal grandmother placing them in an earthen pot and covering them up with bran.

She explained this was necessary to clean out their gastrointestinal systems. I needn't worry; she assured me. They would be happy eating the bran for twenty-four hours, quite unaware of their impending doom.

To have imagined then that one day I would see snails ready-cooked in a tin, with their empty shells held in a net bag on top. My grandmother would never have believed it.

We cooked them with garlic or onions, whichever happened to be available at the time. Indeed, garlic is still used as a sauce in Greece, although few people in the village today have any yearning to sample such a delicacy now because no one is hungry any more.

Retribution was inevitable: it always is. And it arrived at a snail's pace, many decades later. Their progeny assailed me indirectly. Snails, though not of the edible variety, are now avenging the demise of their kin by attacking my delphiniums. They come out at night, stealthily and determined, and devour the tender plants just as they emerge from their earthy cradle. They have been eating the leaves of my hollyhocks, too, those of the sunflowers and even the runner beans that spring from my English soil. How can they chew so well without teeth? Nothing now deters them, only death by chemicals, which is hardly an ecologically friendly solution: but what is one to do?

Snail gourmets may rejoice at those meals of long ago but the very thought of such a repast turns me off food altogether now. It was what we had to do, take our food where we could find it. And Mamma could even find our lunch below the sea.

Sea anemones are like pretty flowers with iridescent fronds. They look like miniature jelly fish, with the same ability to inject an irritant. They are stuck firmly to submerged rocks, awaiting a passing meal in the form of a tiny shrimp or fish, but with a sharp knife it is possible to remove them intact, although care must be taken to avoid contact with the fronds.

Retrieved from the sea, the anemones were tossed in rye flour then fried in olive oil and proved very acceptable to our palates, which is to say, acceptable in 1943, when there was very little else for the table. Husks from the gritty rye, however, pricked our gums and drew blood, and I wonder now what damage was done to our

116

gastrointestinal tracks. Was my early diet the cause of severe gastric problems in middle life? As we had no wheat flour, we had to substitute with rye. I was often given a soup bowl full of it, along with a tablecloth, and sent off to get it ground. I would arrive at the house of Eleni, owner of the mill, where I would spread a cloth on the floor and sit on one corner of it.

The mill, being too heavy to lift, was rolled out: a circular piece of marble with a central wooden pole, the top of the mill having a hole in the centre and a wooden handle on its periphery. The base was placed between my legs; the top was then rolled and put in place over the central pole so that I could pick up handfuls of rye and feed it through the hole. I would grasp the handle with both hands and begin to turn it round counter-clockwise. It was hard work for my arms. I was a skinny twelve-year-old. As the gyrations increased, the mill became so much lighter, easier to control and faster; I would finish in record time. Eleni kindly then removed the mill and I would gather up the cloth, tip the ground rye into it, and return home. Rye flour mixed with wheat was part of our staple diet.

So was black olive paste. Our mother was ahead of her time in that respect.

After peeling two fistfuls of pickled olives and removing the skin and stones, Mamma placed them in a deep plate, drizzled a little olive oil over them and with the back of a spoon, proceeded to mix the olive oil into pulp. The result was a smooth, shiny paste, which looked like chocolate. Spread on bread without butter, we were hardly aware of the existence of butter, tasting salty but quite acceptable. Of course, olive paste, both black and green, is now commercially available.

And if that wasn't sufficient, why, let them eat caviar!—another of our mother's remarkable culinary inventions. Mamma removed the roe from a number of small fish, taking care to separate and discard the gallbladders so that we could not taste the bitterness of the bile. Then she would boil and skin the roes, and as with the olive paste procedure, she had found yet another way to make that heavy brown bread more palatable.

Fish paste too, although very salty, was a most popular and

sought-after foodstuff. Our neighbours would arrive with little jars for a sample. Small fry were salted in order to preserve them; I can still see Mamma with her palm upturned, and on it were arranged the little fish in fives, in a fan shape with heads together at its point. Each fish then joined its fellows, placed in a square tin. Each completed layer was covered with coarse salt. When the container was full, a wooden square was placed on it, and a heavy stone pressed down on the little bodies to ensure their preservation. Mutilation was also the result. In due course, they were removed from their salty preserve, rinsed thoroughly in cold water (or milk if it could be spared), then served on a plate with a little olive oil and vinegar. They were accompanied with bread and were to be eaten when drinking tsipouro (ouzo), distilled grape skins by the men only! Mamma would add only a little oil to the little fish and make a paste by employing her usual method with the back of a spoon.

Of course, we consumed far too much salt but this was inevitable because it was the only available means of preservation, aside from smoking. Bottling of food was unheard of then. Mamma always found ways to feed us, food preparation was only one of her many skills within the family.

Our Goats

"Wake up, my child, wake up! The sun is nearly halfway up the sky. You will miss the herdsman. And you know what that means: there will be no supper tonight or yoghurt tomorrow if that happens!"

The herdsman waited patiently every morning for all the goats at the north end of the village by a dry ditch close to the sea. It was a part of the village that has long since been levelled. Two restaurants are built there now, popular with the tourists, serving fish and other seafood. But not when I was small.

Poor Grandma Evgenia! How many times she had to call me I cannot tell, but it was difficult for me to wake up properly. I was glued to the mattress after a night of torment inflicted by the voracious, blood-sucking bedbugs. Every night was the same; tiny little bugs crawling out of their nooks and crannies as soon as the oil lamp was extinguished, crawling on the skin, sinking their pernicious fangs like vampires. Every night, scratching, tossing, turning, slapping at random, waking smeared with my own blood and sick with the stench.

Welcome rosy dawn, messenger of the sun's reflected light, banishing the enemy and leaving me to relax at last, deeply into sweetly uninterrupted sleep. Deeper and deeper into the arms of Morpheus I snuggled, so that even the crowing cocks, the braying donkeys and the barking dogs could not hope to disturb me. Only the gentle voice of Grandma to wake me up.

And when I woke, the goats!

We had two goats then, a mother and a daughter. The mother was named Bijou and was difficult to control, always darting away

119

in search of more to munch. She had an insatiable appetite. The daughter was known as Pipitsou; she was obedient, never strayed, and followed me like a dog. Both animals were so beautiful! Their coats were black, and on their faces, two white lines started at the top of their heads, between their horns, and traced all the way down to their mouths and chins, with just a splash of black on the nose. Their eyes and eyelids were dark brown, and two pairs of black fleshy appendages under their chins swung from side to side as the goats trotted along.

They were workers and pets at the same time. They greeted us always with "beeheheh!" We always responded in that same language. In the village, there was very little left for them to graze upon. Already, as only goats can, they had devoured all the grass and every sign of greenery. Some had even been known to chew up old shoes or fish bones. Lack of water meant that there were barely enough greens about for humans to consume, let alone for goats. Eventually, they had to be grazed elsewhere. So, it was necessary to take the animals to the herdsman in good time in the morning, and then collect them in the evening, when, as soon as they returned, they would be milked by my Grandma.

As the eldest of my siblings, the job of goat delivery had been delegated to me. I knew the goats well; they had become my friends. So, I was much disturbed when a family of strangers arrived in our village, sheltering from wartime bombing inland, and a man of that family very nearly killed our beautiful Pipitsou.

Once, and this was entirely out of character, the docile Pipitsou darted away from me, straight through the hedge of a nearby garden, and at once began to eat all the lettuces there with speed and relish, entirely ignoring my calls to cease and desist. The stranger appeared at once, seemingly out of nowhere, shouting, swearing and kicking at the poor animal's abdomen repeatedly, making a terrible drum-like sound. My poor Pipitsou must have been full, less of grass than of gas. I was paralysed with fear and simply rooted to the ground in terror. I could no longer find a way to speak or move as he continued kicking and yelling at the animal. I thought that my Pipitsou would die on the spot!

Then, suddenly, he thrust her back through the hedge, practically on top of my squatting, quaking self. A very subdued and weakly bleating animal trotted beside me as we walked back home. I was still crying as I spoke to Grandma between sobs of the disaster that had almost befallen us.

Bijou, the mother, on the other hand, often displayed a wild spirit and was constantly in trouble. She could be totally disobedient and very hard to handle. She would dash off leaving me to chase after her without much hope of really bringing her to heel. It kept Grandma waiting and would often make the milking late.

I will always remember one particular evening when Bijou's lead slipped through my fingers and she ran off like a hound in the very opposite direction to our house. I released Pipitsou and rushed after Bijou to find that she was eating the only patch of grass left in front of Melpo's house. I picked up her lead, pulled, tugged, spoke to her urgently–spoke to her coaxingly. She made no response simply continued her greedy munching. Then a spontaneous thought struck me. I climbed on to her back twisted her ears round her horns and Presto!–I was giving myself a goat ride to the great amusement of everyone who witnessed me riding her home. I was the hero of the day.

By the age of fourteen, my goat-herding days were prematurely over. I had left the village to go to school in Thessaloniki. Nevertheless, I never forgot my goats; they were my pets, after all. When I ultimately learned what had happened to them in my absence I was deeply upset. Bijou had died from old age, which was neither unexpected nor tragic. But sadly Pipitsou had died too during a very severe and prolonged winter when wolves and jackals descended in the night attacking many animals. Even a donkey was mauled by the ghastly creatures. My Pipitsou had been sleeping in her usual place by the big oven in the shed when a jackal had taken a bite out of her milk sack. Infection set in at once and in spite of warm bathing and poultices, the infection persisted and killed her.

There was no veterinary surgeon then no doctor or medicines for people let alone for our animals. All were doomed if they fell seriously ill. It was just something else one had to be patient about.

The Journey

"There go Mary and Joseph!" exclaimed the farmers and shepherds who gathered to see us off.

But it was not December; it was the middle of summer. The fierce heat of the sun made everything around us shimmer: vision dazzled; all sound seemed suppressed. Life was taking a siesta—only the cicadas could defy the holocaust. Clinging fast to branches, they would further enhance our mood for sleep by their monotonous and soporific song. In that oppressive heat, Vassili and I felt very cold.

We were about to have an attack of malaria. I cannot remember who arranged the transport to our village from Servikon. However, I do remember sitting on the saddle of a donkey where Vassili joined me. A blue blanket held us together for warmth and stability.

It was this tableau that provoked the onlookers' comments. But this Mary and Joseph were not going to Bethlehem to be taxed according to the decree of Caesar (St. Luke, Chapter 2, and Verse 1). Indeed, this Joseph was not on foot, for he too was riding the donkey. This Mary wasn't heavy with child but simply a thirteen-year-old girl burdened with "the Holy Ghost" of infected blood.

The boy Vassili was older than me. We were both in the throes of a malarial attack: the onset is a fever characterised by headaches and joint pains. Rigor sets in thereafter, and the muscular system goes into uncontrollable spasm, causing shivering and a gnashing of teeth. This all culminates in a high temperature, which is the body's defence against the killer invader. Nausea and delirium then take over.

I have few recollections of that journey at all, beyond what I have told you. Who lifted us into the saddle? Who led the donkey to the village? I have no memory of arriving at our house. Was I lifted from my mount or did I dismount by myself?

What I remember to this day is how cold I felt in the midst of that blazing summer sun. My mother held my shaking body and tried to reassure me through the haze of my illness.

"Mamma, pile more bedding on me and press down hard."

But it made little difference until the temperature reached such a high degree that the body became its own oven.

I came to consciousness overwhelmed by a wave of nausea. I was on a makeshift bed outside under the vine. My mother was bent over me supporting my head. I was distressed with retching and crying and between sobs, I kept repeating to Mamma, "I don't mind the fever. Please stop the nausea!" As if she could.

When exhaustion led to sleep, my dream was always the same. I was attempting to cut a paploma (a duvet-like thick bed covering) with a pair of very fine and delicate embroidery scissors. Needless to say that, hard as I tried even by gritting my teeth and grasping the scissors, I simply failed to make any advance. As my dream continued, it returned me to Servikon, where the cause of my illness (the mosquitoes) and the onset of the infection had begun. I was on my way to the supposed running stream near our property. Of course, none existed. I must have felt thirsty, in need of a drink, and was dreaming of clean fresh water. I woke up to find myself in bed.

The side effects of malaria for me were: loss of weight, general weakness and jaundice—the result of the destruction by larvae of the red blood cells. It took me a very long time to recover, but I did. Poor Vassili died.

Many families went to Servikon in the summer. It was an area of the country on the opposite side of the peninsula from our village. We went there to work and to guard our allotments. We grew melons and sweet corn. Drinking water in Servikon had to be fetched from a spring some distance away from our field. Steliani, my friend and neighbour, would join me. We were the water carriers for our respective families. We would set off with our buckets in the comparative coolness of the late afternoon. Our path lay between thickets of ferns under a canopy of trees that cut out much of the light: this was an ideal environment for the mosquito population. On our left was a ditch with a thick layer of green algae. The water was stagnant: it never rippled or rolled. This made it a haven for dragonflies and mosquitoes. As we ambled along, we enjoyed pushing the ferns aside to broaden our path and amused ourselves by unfurling their tightly curled feathery fronds to watch them spring back to their intricate motifs. In so doing, we disturbed whole clouds of mosquitoes, which normally waited for the light to fade before visiting our quarters in their hundreds to gorge on our blood and regurgitate parasites that caused malaria.

We slept in open-air makeshift shelters without any protection from barrier creams or mosquito nets. So, within a month of arrival at Servikon, a family usually would be nursing a child or an adult—more usually a child. There was no treatment other than the relief of symptoms. My mother must have felt helpless. All she could do was keep vigil over me, put compresses of water and vinegar on my forehead and other parts of my hot body to relieve the fever.

In 1945, antiprine and quinine were finally introduced to our village. We disliked swallowing the bitter pills, though at least these caused no pain. The injections of quinine were extremely painful. However, only one could be spared for me. In fact, the best treatment was DDT. It was sprayed by helicopter on all the stagnant waters and by hand held atomisers on all of us and the inside of our houses also. DDT became popular, almost a fashion. It was easily obtained and indiscriminately used, just as antibiotics were later. Both have now lost their so-called magic. But after their use, summer in Servikon became much less of an ordeal.

THE LOG CABIN

In Sevrikon our father constructed a summer house for us: A house on stilts. Our pet goats Bijou and Pipitsou occupied the ground floor. The humans (us) lived and slept on the first slatted floor above them, comforted and oddly reassured by their noisily intimate exchanges and their munching below. The log cabin was an ideal setting for us. We were isolated there often left without our father who would mostly be away with his friends hunting wild boar. We climbed the rungs barefoot gripping them with curled toes because they were roughly circular tree-branches; father had brought only his big saw along so the wood remained in its natural shape.

We slept on the wooden floor which was well cushioned with woven rugs made from strips of old clothes (recycling was common practice then) topped by a thick tserya–a shepherd's ground cover. Here we shared these open sleeping quarters not with the bedbugs that plagued us at home but with malaria-infected mosquitoes. The lice became our lesser enemies for once not least because our clothing was reduced to a minimum. I wore a pink shift with knickers to match which our clever mother had made from an old petticoat. This made me feel very cool and happy as there were few hiding places there for the lice or at least so I hoped.

I was celebrating the freedom from body lice when one day I discovered one of my old foes: a louse on my body. It was such an unexpected and disappointing shock.

This was how I discovered what felt to me like an assault upon my person. The outdoor toilet was behind any bush at a distance from our living space to provide certain privacy. I squatted and began to relieve myself and as I cast an idle but curious glance at the urine streaming along, my attention strayed to my pubic area. There to my horror and mounting distress I saw a long bloated louse crawling and wobbling in the sparse undergrowth of my nascent hair!

I feel a nausea in my throat at even the memory of it!

The shock interrupted the stream at once. I grasped the offending intruder between finger and thumb and squeezed it hard to disable it.

I clench my teeth even now as I write of it!

With my knickers now almost round my ankles, I found two stones nearby, and placing the lousy creature on one surface, I pulverised it with the other rock until only a small brown stain was visible. Then I felt sick with revulsion and humiliation, but I was quite unable to tell Mamma about it. I knew instinctively that my mother would not have approved of my activities: watching the distance of neither my stream of urine nor my curiosity at the growth of pubic hair.

At school we would often measure the streams of urine. The toilets were in a ditch about sixty metres away from the building, the girls' to the left, the boys' to the right, a footpath crossing the ditch between us. There of course it was a competition. And we had to squat far enough from one another so that our outstretched arms couldn't reach those of our friends. Contact had to be avoided at all costs because if fingers touched it was said that our mothers would in the future, produce not little children but baby hares. One had to take such things seriously back then.

I took my secret back to the cabin with me and left the louse dead upon a stone to tell no tales.

SUICIDE

The inner intimate silken leaves of maize, which hug the cones studded with the golden kernels, lend themselves to mat and basket-making; that it to say they did indeed for me in childhood. Little nimble fingers would tear the leaves lengthwise to finger-width, then tie them into bunches of a dozen or so. They were often dyed in vibrant colours. The thickness of the bunches was determined by the proposed item to be fashioned. The common thickness used by children was the size of a female adult finger. One of the strips would be used as a bandage, to hold together a bunch of the strips and make a flexible rope. This is the humble beginning of all items to be made from the stuff.

The rope has to be continuously lengthened by adding more of the strips when only a quarter of its original size is left. The only tool we used apart from the hands was a hairpin. It takes time and perseverance to get the knack of the art and craft of creating mats and baskets. Starting with the flexible rope: fold the end on itself a couple of times, holding it together. Then, take a strip, wind it firmly round the free part of the rope, insert the hairpin in the centre of it, thread it, and pull it through. The next step is to thread the hairpin to pull through the strip, bring it out to the free end of the rope and continue as at the beginning. It is many decades since I practiced the craft therefore I hesitate to recommend my own instructions.

I learned how to make tablemats by watching other children and adults of our neighbourhood during summer afternoons. We sat outside in the shade, watched the activities and listened to the grown-ups gossiping. We then elaborated on the items discussed, adding our own interpretations to the mix. It was best not to let the adults here our versions of their tales.

It was quite easy to make a round table mat; I had already succeeded in that line early on. I imagine it would have been within my capability to undertake an ovoid shape and weave a basket. And so I declared my intention to all present but I was very disappointed with a chorus of, "You will never finish it. It is too soon for you to undertake such a difficult shape."

I would have none of it of course and embarked on a marathon of slow progress. It was three knots forward and two knots backwards. What actually frustrated me was getting the shape of it to look like an ovoid, like a ship, but it looked more like a man's slipper trodden down at the heel. Of course, everyone who had warned me said so, in no uncertain terms, and laughed at me to my face.

Mamma was not very encouraging. She kept telling me that the basket was misshapen and that I must unpick it and either finish it or give it up. She said it was too hideous to have it brought out every afternoon after making so little progress. The shape Mamma said was a disgrace. And that was the "straw that broke the camel's back." How could our mother offend me in front of my peers and neighbours? This was totally out of character on her part: Mamma usually praised me. Yet, only the day before, she had hit me on the mouth with the back of her hand. Her wedding ring made a resounding tingling sound on my teeth. It was about my hair, which was not very long yet. Mamma hoped that by the time the war was over, and my godfather, who liked my hair long, returned it would reach my shoulders. I said that I would pull on my two plaits to encourage them to grow quickly: that invited the back hander. I was utterly humiliated and in pain from the impact the wedding ring had on my lips and teeth.

I responded with a threat: I was going to drown myself!

Had Mamma forgotten all the other jobs I was good at? Well, now I would teach her a lesson, just see if I didn't! I stood up purposefully, threw my much-criticised work on the bench that I shared with family and friends and departed.

What did I look like in my haste to reach the sea? I imagine my wooden footwear would have raised a trail of dust behind me and the scraping noise it made on the stony parts of the road would have made some people look in my direction and wonder at the nature of my mission in the heat of the day.

The stones and pebbles were very hot. I wobbled over them and reached the edge of the shore. I undressed, put down my clothes with my clogs beside them and crept away to hide by the hedge. I was in no doubt that if I had not returned within a short interval a frightened Mamma would come along looking for me. The sea was only three houses away to the south. Sure enough, Mamma arrived and stood very near me without noticing me. She searched the deserted beach and then spied the little neat pile of my possessions, all as planned. She went right up to the water's edge and looked out to the sea.

What happened next?

Well, I called to her in a very trembling voice and expected a severe telling-off, but nothing of the sort happened. Our poor mother must have been so relieved to see me alive that she was lost for words: she didn't reproach me in the least.

I have often thought about this incident over the years but cannot remember whether I took all my clothes off or why Mamma chose to humiliate me in front of neighbours. I feel guilty for my unforgivable behaviour even now.

What drives a child, for I was no more than ten to eleven years old, to think such things and to threaten to end its life? The factors were numerous in my case, including a sudden need to grow up following the arrival of the latest sibling. It exacerbated our mother's already fragile health. Consequently, it altered the balance of domestic work, increasing the load on Grandma and adding an extra dimension to mine by giving me responsibility in the care of the new baby. I thought of myself as a little mother at the early age of ten. Yet, I still had a driving need for my mother—I needed to be her baby from time to time, and the mother-infant conflict welled up inside me until I had to play out a drama that forced my mother to once again cradle me in her arms.

Our School

It was a wooden rectangular building divided into three areas: a large hall and two small rooms facing east. The teacher had one of the small rooms as his office, the other was a storeroom. There were no washing facilities or lavatories. We made use of a dry ditch a little distance from the school. The girls went to the left, the boys to the right side; just in the same order as in the village church. And, of course, there was no paper such as we have now. A tuft of grass sufficed—less abrasive than the taw: a raffia-like fibre for cleaning incontinent patients' nether-regions. Taw was used because the government toilet paper was non-absorbent. I came across this material when I was a student nurse in the UK, though I once knew a girl from Nea Rhoda who used a little pointed stone...

No, we didn't wash our hands; there wasn't any running water in the ditch. I do remember the talk of the previous year's tomato seedlings though. We joked among ourselves in scatological terms for this unusual way of sowing tomatoes. Of course, we swore we would never eat the produce!

Summertime was too hot to pay any attention to lessons. The exasperated teacher had no control over us and would throw us out on to the playground, which was simply a dust bowl. Once outside we drifted home to enforced siestas.

Winter in a wooden building, on the other hand, was extremely cold for all the children, but most especially those whose desks were distant from the wood burning stove. This massive beast was a large black contraption with a round opening at its top for feeding it with wood. Keeping it fed was the teacher's job, naturally. Just below the top and to the side emerged a short funnel: it twisted into an elbow-like joint and climbed towards the ceiling, where it stopped short, made another elbow-like joint and eased itself through a ready-made hole in the wall to the outside world. Another and final twist sent a short funnel upwards. It was capped with a cowl, which looked like a plate on stilts. Its function was to stop the rain and wind from intruding down the pipe. At a much lower level of the stove was an opening with a little door. This was for removing the cinders at the end of the day and laying the fire ready for the next: another task for the teacher. The pupils sitting on the long sides of the classroom were exposed to more heat than those whose desks were situated at the east and west positions. To maintain a comfortable environment, the stove had to be fed frequently by the teacher. Winter over, the stove was dismantled and stored away in the other small room.

I had been a pupil there for three years when the war started. No more school for six years. I remember only two separate lessons: attempting to form the letters of the alphabet and getting stuck on letter Delta. I wrote the capital–it is simple enough. However, the lower case was difficult. I drew a zero between the two parallel lines, added a vertical line, extended it to the top line and finished with a flourish, dragging it to the right to make it look like a walking stick resting on a ball. The teacher's remarks elude me.

Not so in religious instruction. The one lesson I recall was about Jacob's ladder to reach God in Heaven.

"Draw Jacob's ladder children."

I drew two parallel lines at an angle and positioned them against a lot of fluffy clouds. I added stick figures of men on different rungs. I was downcast and disappointed when the teacher declared in a voice for all to hear that it was a poor representation. It was unfair, of course, but the artist was already in the third year of primary school but should have done better. Is it a wonder, then, that when my English was still a foreign language, I referred to myself as "artless" when asked if I was artistic?

Disruption in the classroom was common. Some of the older boys were prone to be violent and ready to fight with fists and kicks during lessons. It must have been a very stressful time for the teacher, especially when he had to intervene. I do remember very vividly when a senior boy (he couldn't have been more than twelve years old, but looked nearly as tall as the teacher) was made to stand in the corner near the office as punishment for threatening another boy with a pruning knife, having a curved serrated blade for pruning the vines. When the teacher asked him to surrender his weapon, he actually tried to attack him!

Each morning we queued in crocodile fashion for inspection before lessons could begin. The teacher looked at our hair, faces and hands. On one such occasion my little sisters, Evgenia and Angeliki, no more than six years, looked unwashed and their hair needed attention. I don't remember the reason for this. It could have been at the time Grandma was out of action due to her broken shoulder, and Mamma was ill because of her asthma. I was called to the front of the queue and asked to present my hands with palms facing up. I knew then what was coming to me. He raised the hand holding the ruler and brought it down on my palms, first on one and then the other. He justified his action by telling all present that my sisters' appearance was my fault. As an older sister (by seventeen months), I should have attended to my siblings' appearance.

The poor man had no choice but to rule by his ruler.

THE GRAPE HARVEST

This autumn was to be the last year of school for me and all the other children in our village. I was in my third year of primary learning and would not be sitting at a school bench again for six long years. On that particular morning, I was on my way to the classroom via the vineyard. Grandma took me with her. I cannot remember the reason for this: possibly to prune the vines. As we approached the village, the church bell began to toll in a most urgent and vigorous manner, unlike any tolling we were accustomed to. All public and domestic events were thus announced in our village: For a wedding, the ringing was vibrant, happy and cheerful; in the case of a funeral, it was a dirge - a slow mournful noise that brought the people out of their homes asking the inevitable question from their neighbour or passer-by: "Who has passed away?" We were at war! No school! Let the children rejoice and the parents despair. However, we missed the schoolroom where we could be just children—despite the frequent caning by the teacher. That poor man had to control the entire population of seven- to twelve-year-old children in one classroom, after all. And, he had to do it all by himself.

Mostly, Grandma and Mamma (when free from her medical condition) cared for our vineyard. It had to be hoed, and I helped along with the adults. Mamma was clever and fast at pruning. When the first leaves began to emerge from the hard branches, Grandma was on the lookout for possible pests. She would be ready with the sulphur-charged atomizer to dust the leaves and the flowers as they emerged looking infested. To encourage a good and generous crop it was essential to remove some of the foliage. I do not recollect any pruning of the flowers; though, when the actual grapes formed compacted clusters, some of the fruit was removed to encourage the size of the remainder. We longed for the summer to hurry up and bring along the hot sun to ripen the grapes and other fruits so that we could feast on them.

Right in the middle of the vineyard was a pear tree. The fruit was delicious. We always made a beeline for it and the fig tree on the periphery. The bees, wasps and fruit-eating beetles were there long before us - Grandma would always say the insects arrive with the sunrise. One insect was a brilliant emerald in colour - it never failed to dazzle us when the bright sun's rays settled on its carapace. It actually looked like an Egyptian scarab. We were fascinated by its brilliance. We longed to possess one and use it as a plaything, a toy. I have a sense of guilt about it now, even after so many decades. I remember how we would climb the tree and look for the beautiful beetle feeding on one of the ripest pears unaware of its imminent capture and torture. One of us would hold it firmly but without undue pressure to avoid damage, whist the other child tied a thread round the thorax. The dominant hand then held the remaining length of thread tightly. Ready—steady—go! We would run as if trailing a kite and swing the captive fast in a circular motion, which forced the unfortunate scarab to fly. This was a great achievement for us; it was exhilarating and very exciting. I am sorry to admit now that it amused and gratified us greatly. What an awfully cruel way to treat one of nature's treasured creatures! And, that is not the worst of it. When our captive died—as it inevitably did—we kept it as a trophy. We knew no better. We had no toys; we were forced to be inventive. But unfortunately it was often at the expense of helpless creatures.

Last May, while I was living in Ouranoupolis, I was brought up short when one of those emerald beetles alighted on the balcony in front of me. It was such an unexpected and emotional incident. I chose to take it as an omen of forgiveness. The scarab beetle was always referred to as the "Ginjikas." We sang a tongue twister as children that declared him to be a thief who climbed up the Ginjiria (pear tree) and ate the ginjira (pears):

Oh, Ginjiras, oh Minjiras,
Oh, Ginjiminjiconjiras,
Anaevike stin Ginjiria,

134

Stin Ginjiminjikojiria,
Kae effaye, ta Ginjira,
Ta Minjira, ta ginjiminjiconjira!

I remember, too, the boys in our neighbourhood kicking a "ball," which was actually an inflated pig's bladder. That was inventive and enterprising indeed. The animal had to be killed to provide food anyway, so it was not sacrificed specifically to provide a toy. This was just one of many ways we availed ourselves of the delights that could be provided by certain unfortunate creatures.

We made many visits to the vineyard to collect grapes in order to have them with bread and cheese. for our meals: bread and grapes were a popular snack. We also checked the general ripeness of the grapes for the harvest. This was a very rewarding task indeed. It provided us the opportunity to gorge our greedy little selves: we consumed more than we picked. The recollections of pick-your-own days remind me of strawberry picking on Dax farm in Kent with my children. It was one of those rare days when the sun threw hot rays to our world and the air was scented with ripe strawberries. The singing sky larks floated overhead, suspended in the sky like a young child's mobile.

The thought transports me to my village now as I write. On one day in particular, Grandma and I were hoeing the melon patch when I saw a bird hovering and singing over us. I hadn't noticed it ever before.

"Grandma, why is that bird hanging in the sky just over one spot?"

"That little bird is waiting for us to move away, and then it will fly down to its nest," she replied.

"On the earth? Is it not afraid of snakes?"

I for one was absolutely terrified of the dastardly creatures. I certainly didn't consider it a safe place for a bird's nest!

That same very warm spring day, Nico, one of our young male neighbours, was also busy very close to us. He suddenly called out, "Yiayia! Come and see what I have just dug up!" (The young often addressed old ladies thus, Yiayia being another word for Grandma.)

135

It was a clutch of cream-coloured eggs he had found. They looked velvety with circular ridges. Compared to hens' eggs they were more like what pullets would produce.

"Do cover them up immediately, my boy, before they get cold" advised Grandma. They were tortoise eggs. Tortoises were a common sight in my childhood, though unfortunately not any more.

Now I shall return to the vineyard. The harvesting was in progress and we were urged to gather–rather than eat–the fruit. Once the crop was in the panniers it had to be transported home, some by donkey and the rest on foot, by everyone participating in the harvest. The accompanying adults ignored our moans and groans. However, for all of our complaints, the thought of treading the grapes on the morrow moved our tired little feet homeward purposefully and cheerfully. The vat was brought into the oven shed and set on two sturdy plinths; an upturned wooden box served as a step for the adults. I don't remember climbing into it myself, nor do I recollect washing my feet before the stomping began. The yeast fermentation did a good job in eliminating the bacteria, regardless of what lie under the nails of our toes. Of course, none of this would have crossed my mind at that time.

Inside the oven shed, the wasps soon located the vat and the tap. They became docile very quickly as a result of drinking up the moustos: (the first draught, it is sweet and intoxicating) from the tap. I was extremely happy treading the grapes: the squelching noise I made was great fun. The squashed fruit oozed through my toes; it was a tickling sensation that brought a giggle from my throat. It was like fine wet sand between the toes at the seaside, but with fruit pulp, it was smoother and more sensuous. The wasps were not the only ones affected by the intoxicating air, I shouldn't wonder.

The moustos was eventually poured into a couple of small barrels to mature and become wine. A quantity was set aside in a heavy preserving pan for petimezi. This preserve is made with pumpkin or squash. The fruit is cut in rectangles of two finger lengths and thickness, boiled in the grape moustos until it becomes transparent and golden. It is then stored in earthen glazed containers and sealed. It will be eaten during the long fast before Easter or on any other fasting days. In reality, the amount available to each household is dictated by a good crop of grapes. When plentiful, it would be offered to visitors. However, when only a limited quantity was made, it was reserved for us to use in the winter months. We ate it with bread for breakfast and for tea.

My childhood experience with grape fermentation was truly a memorable affair. I was sitting on the balcony one evening in my adulthood, enjoying the balmy twilight, when my attention was drawn to a very loud bubbling-like noise. The smell of moustos, the grape juice, dripping out of the vat permeated the evening air and drifted over me like warm memories. I had seen my brother Byron the previous evening across the garden harvesting his Georgian grape vine. He had put the grapes in a small vat, pressed them down with his hands and followed with a round piece of wood, like a breadboard. On top of this, he placed what seemed a very heavy stone by the way he was carrying it. He must have fetched it from the seashore, just fifty metres from his front door. This kept the pressure on the fruit. Within twenty-four hours, fermentation must have been remarkably and loudly established to have reached me from his yard across the way. The promise of a forgotten delicacy awaited me in the days to come.

EASTER

Easter is the great festival of the spring. I remember the countryside suddenly alive with bird song and wild flowers, carpets of red poppies as red as Christ's blood to remind the people of his sacrifice for their sake. Camomile and anemones covered the fallow fields as the sun climbed ever higher into the broad blue sky. The honey bees arrived buzzing, making for the camomile flowers, so that walking barefoot in the fields was a hazard, but we did it nevertheless back then and much enjoyed that sweet-scented experience. Nowadays, can children find pleasure any longer in such simple pursuits? Who can persuade the present generation of youth to discard their trainers and wade in the tender grass of the camomile fields?

Easter is simply the most important ecclesiastical celebration of the Orthodox Church. It is preceded by forty days of fasting to remind the faithful of the Forty Days that Jesus spent in the wilderness. As children, we fasted for those entire forty days, although today it seems that a week is what the majority observe. The sick, the very old and very young, the pregnant and lactating women were then as now exempt from this requirement. And in the old days the fasting diet was very simple: black bread, black olives (for it was too early in the year for the green variety), black tea harvested from the mountains with just a little sugar, and a variety of beans and chickpeas soaked overnight and boiled the next day for what seemed hours. A small quantity of olive oil was permitted in the cooking only three times a week. We all looked a little too thin, especially the children. As a child, I could point out the only person who always looked big and round: the local priest. I remember Grandma telling us of a priest who had travelled with her family by sea during Lent. He kindly offered some of his haricot-bean soup to the party, who found it very tasty. Did the Holy Father bless it? "No, my children, I have to confess that the meal was prepared with chicken stock by my dear wife." Greek orthodox priests are blessed with marriage; but it must take place before induction into priesthood.

Church services dominate Lent. For forty days, the priests of the Orthodox Church carry them out twice a day. The Church bells call the faithful each morning and evening to attend and worship. Church protocol demands the men occupy the right side of the House of God and that women take their position on the left. In the old days when I was a child, most of us answered the call to worship. Now however, the regular attendants are just a few old men and some, mostly elderly, women who arrive at the beginning of the services and see it through to the end. Some middle-aged mothers also join the congregation halfway through. During the last week of Lent, even nowadays, the congregation swells little by little to include more of the old males and females, and boys and girls.

On Megali Wednesday ("Great Wednesday") of Holy Week, eggs are dyed red to signify the blood of Christ. Then, on Megali Thursday, the Easter bread is made. Its ingredients these days are: flour, sugar, butter, eggs, milk, various spices and just a pinch of salt. The dough is kneaded into elaborate plaits and baked in (now common) modern electric ovens. It's an aroma that pervades the entire village and is simply delicious. But of course, it should not be eaten until after the Day of Resurrection, even though the temptation is very great, and there are always one or two persons unable to resist—just ensuring the recipe was accurately followed, of course!

On this day, too, the young women adorn the Epitaphios—a wooden structure not unlike a child's cot on waist-high legs, or indeed a four-poster bed, where a life-size icon of Christ Jesus lay. A ceiling and a canopy above it represent His tomb. When I was a child, the flowers for the Epitaphios came from the village gardens. I joined other children going from door to door with open panniers asking for blooms. Mostly wallflowers, but also aromatic pale pink carnations and sometimes some equally well-scented roses.

The entire structure, apart from the legs that were covered by a white valance, was then covered with the flowers: a splendid sight,

139

most pleasing to the eye. The wax smell of the burning candles mingled with the heady scents of the flowers. Now, the flowers arrive in refrigerated vans. They are white and red chrysanthemum forced to blossom early, then arrested to look like daisies of the same size, about that of a ten pence coin. Each bloom is decapitated, a dressmaker's pin driven through its little heart and pinned to a polystyrene panel for the artist to copy her designs from the selected pattern.

I joined the group of young women a couple of years ago in my advanced age, much to their amusement and gratitude. I did this because I was not in my village during my years as a young woman. I had never had the pleasure of participating in this part of the event. The Epitaphios is a much-admired work of art. However, it now lacks the freshness of spring evoked by the wallflowers of the olden days.

Now, let me take you back to the waxy smell of burning candles and incense smouldering and smoking in the thuirible as the priest swung it rhythmically to and fro, creating an ambience, which truly took one out of oneself. I would look at what was for my years the mighty height of the vault and imagine angels flying round the painted image of the Pantocrator who looked down upon us, and I'd wonder if God might be cross with me at all, for all my misdemeanours.

Megali Friday (Good Friday), is the saddest day of that Holy Week, being the day of the Crucifixion. After the evening service, follows the procession through the village. Four young men lift the Epitaphios aloft, shoulder-high, and exit the church with the priest at the head, followed by the throng carrying simple lit wax candles. The priest swings the incense thuirible and intones more of the service. The sleeping village pays its respects to the Epitaphios by placing lighted candles at open windows or with traditional home burners smouldering with incense. The priest stops at each corner; he continues to intone the sufferings of Christ, and eventually all return to Church, the people go home, the Epitaphios is placed in front of the Temple and the icon of the crucified Christ is then fixed to a man-size cross at the top end of the Church centre.

Sophia, one of my cousins with a lovely voice, kept vigil with me on this occasion and with the other women parishioners,

140

kneeling and sitting at the foot of the cross. Sophia led the singing appropriate for the sacred occasion. It is a very moving experience. When the parishioners decide to leave, they cross themselves, kneel at the foot of the cross, kiss the feet of Jesus, walk backwards for a few steps and go out into the dark night or early morning on their way home.

Megalo Sabbato (Great Saturday), the last day of Lent reaches the climax of Christ's suffering. The bell tolls mournfully at eleven o'clock in the evening. The parishioners arrive in twos and threes. Some wait by the entrance to the House of God before entering with family and friends. The church overflows with celebrants, who spill out on the periphery. The throng swells by visitors staying in the local hotels and by other Greeks who make the journey all the way from Thessaloniki. Many carry beautifully decorated candles to receive the Light from the priest during the final part of the service. By this time, everyone is holding Easter candles. At the stroke of twelve midnight, the priest proclaims: "Receive Light-thefte lavete fos," stepping out of the temple on the female side, offering the light from his candle. One person approaches reverently, lights her candle, and from then on the light spreads to all the candle holders. The priest returns to the temple and emerges from the master archway to proclaim further the Resurrection of Christ. Then, he and the faithful sing loudly and cheerfully, "Christos anesti ek nekron thanato thanaton patisssas kai tis enti mnimati, zoin harisamenos!" [Christ is risen from the dead having triumphed over death and given life to those who have died]. Fireworks streak the clear and starry sky, all rejoicing but hungry, turning their steps homeward for the welcoming magiritsa.

The priest must surely be exhausted by this time—he's conducted eighty services in forty days, as well as other inevitable duties such as funerals, which have to be conducted within twenty-four hours of expiring, as the village has no facilities for keeping the dead safely. No doubt, the priest encourages good health during Lent. Easter Sunday dawns then, too early for him after such a short night. Nevertheless, he looks resplendent in his gold and silver embroidered vestments, waiting there in the inner temple with the altar boys also splendidly dressed in long red garments beneath their pristine white surplices. Very few parishioners respond to that joyous first bell. It is usually only the elderly who are there, the ones

141

who wake up at the crack of dawn and cannot get back to sleep. But by midday, the church fills up to capacity and the psalmists intone in response to the reading of the gospels and the epistles by the priest. The service is completed by a second procession around the village before the faithful disperse and go home to dine on roasted Paschal Lamb or goat on the spit.

I remember those simpler times. Nowadays the Easter meal is like a banquet: the dining tables are groaning under the weight of food. Apart from the main course, there are dishes such as roasted meats of lamb, goat, and kokoretsi, made with internal organs threaded on like a giant kebab, secured with lengths of intestines and roasted: another delicacy which I leave well alone. There'll be tsipouro, wines, beers and Coca Cola, Greek salads, salted fish, plain bread, feta cheese, olives, red eggs and couloures. The men begin the meal by drinking the tsipouro accompanied by the salted fish, olives in olive oil and oreganon, by feta cheese with a drizzle of the same, or by sweet red roasted peppers. Whilst the men eat well and get merry, the wives and daughters are all on foot supplying more food and drink before sitting down to their own well-earned meals.

Our family home remains, as it always has been, in close proximity to the village church. The service is clearly audible from outside our back door under the vine. It could be effortlessly followed and Mamma often did so when the weather permitted, preferring the outdoors, as her breathing felt easier. Mamma was a believer. However, she had resisted asking God to cure her of her debilitating illness—chronic bronchial asthma. Then in her late fifties, she declared to my sister, Angeliki, (I had long departed to another land by then) that she had decided to fast and pray for forty days and forty sleepless nights—her asthma allowed her very little sleep—in the hope that in His mercy God would cure her of an affliction that had robbed her of so much in life that she wanted to do. She embarked on earnest prayer, firmly expecting a miracle. She fasted and prayed both audibly and in silence for the entire of Lent. However, at the end of her marathon, Mamma was still suffering as greatly as ever. Between gasps, she announced to Angeliki that God had not chosen to cure her after all. Thus she had lost her faith in the Almighty. She wasn't even sixty years old. She died at sixty-two, too young to die when she had so much to give.

142

The Paschal Lamb in this celebration of the Resurrection was for us no lamb at all, but one of our own beloved goats—a baby goat slaughtered by decapitation, skinned and drawn, washed and stuffed with rice, sultanas and spices. Then it was sewn-up, placed in the circular baking dish we called a tapsi, surrounded with potatoes cut in wedges for the occasion, all ready to be offered to the gaping monster mouth of our white-hot oven, to join all the other Easter victims.

We ate our pet kid goat! Were we upset? We did weep, but we ate the meal anyway. After forty days of fasting, it wasn't like Mamma had to twist our arms to make us eat.

The internal organs of the goats were used also. I remember very well squatting at the edge of the sea shore, the little waves drifting up to wet and tease my toes, the temperature still too cool for wading, as I worked away at the animal's intestines which were destined to be used in the magiritsa. Magiritsa is a traditional soup eaten past midnight after the Resurrection service, when the celebrants all return home with their lighted candles. On reaching the household, the head of the family would trace the sign of the cross at the inside top of the doorframe to ensure the security of the home during the coming year, thus keeping evil thoughts and deeds away. Then the family sit down to that steaming-hot soup, to crack red eggs and to eat the Easter bread. My job was to take a bowlful of the cut-up intestines, in lengths of two hand spans, knot one end and invert it over a stick, its slippery tubular length so recently a part of my pet animal. And did I weep as I sat there beside the waves? No. Why not? Fasting for forty days had blunted my feelings. Were we so hungry for flesh that we could cannibalise our beloved pets, our kid-goats and hens so easily? But isn't this what humans resort to when planes come down on top of snow-covered mountains?

It was a very laborious task. Each length had to be thoroughly rinsed more than once to remove the foetid smell, which was unmistakable despite the fact that the animal had been milk-fed up to the moment of its beheading. Other parts of its anatomy: heart, liver, pancreas, and spleen, were chopped up and added to the intestines, seasoned with salt, pepper and herbs, and boiled up to make the magiritsa. The addition of a beaten egg and the juice of a

143

lemon completed the dish. These two ingredients are beaten together vigorously with a fork until a firm froth has developed, then a ladleful of hot soup is taken and carefully drizzled over the frothy peaks with one hand while the other beats the hot and cold ingredients together until the soup plate is full and frothy. All this is slowly added back to the pot, so that the egg is cooked as it is stirred and is ready to be served as avgolemono, the addition of which disguises any unpleasant thoughts of intestine. I still refuse to eat it.

Easter was and still is full of such specialities—red eggs dyed on Megali Wednesday, couloures or tsourekia, the special Easter bread, always baked on Megali Thursday. When the tsourekia are taken to the village oven for baking. The aroma of this deliciously spiced bread, as it is collected to be taken home, traverses the roads along the way. How difficult it was to prevent the children, and even the grown-ups, from sneaking to the table that supports the tapsi, and breaking off a piece, just to taste its seductive quality! The Paschal Lamb and the kid goats are roasted in the village oven, electrified now, of course, all shining stainless steel, and with tiled flooring: not a trace of cinders. But this popular new system doesn't always produce satisfactory results. When the numbers to be baked exceed the oven's capacity, there is a long delay in baking the couloures, the yeast continues to rise and then flops as it expires, so that by the time they are finally placed in the oven, the dough will not bake as lightly, and the result is disappointing. Even so, not a crumb is left, not after the second day—unless, of course, they have been well hidden. Some things about Easter in the village do not change.

The Holidays

The celebration of Christmas was yet another festival proceeded by fasting and daily church services. As I remember it the children made only a small contribution: the chanting of two pieces dedicated to Mary, the Mother of God. A boy stood on the right, facing up to the Temple, with a girl taking her place on the left likewise. I clearly remember the year when it was I performing my part. As I steadily progressed, more and more of my voice lost its resonance. Nerves, of course. I felt extremely embarrassed. What was worse was that I had let my teacher down. He had chosen me because I had performed so well at rehearsal. However, I did croak on to the end...

In those days, we believed in God and in his wrath. If we were naughty children, we were threatened with Hell and Purgatory. Indeed, we believed in a Devil who could be summoned by adults to carry us off to the pit. One of our neighbours displayed on a wall a full man-sized poster of a scene from Hell—a black cauldron standing over a blazing fire, tongues of savage flames were lashing out of it, and between them lunged demons with horns coming out of their heads, and harpoons poised to attack the wicked. Much later in life, when I studied at Advanced Level in English Literature, I wrote a poem, which goes:

> *Rugged tongues of orange flames ablaze,*
> *Black demons with harpoons poised,*
> *Yellow teeth, their tongues purple,*
> *Standing amongst them*
> *To harpoon the wicked people.*
>
> *We ran fast past it and away:*
> *Demons chase after children*

Who fib and don't pray.

In the cauldron of boiling pitch,
Their barbed harpoons dip,
Awaiting Lucifer's orders
Their infernal pains to inflict.

Of course, we went to church regularly and always recited our prayers at bedtime to keep ourselves safe from the evil one. Does this seem a strange way to remember Christmas? In those days, before and during the Second World War, in our village we had no idea about Christmas as we know it today. It was not just that Easter was the more important festival; little of what we now associate with the Christmas season was available for us back then. To this day, my Greek relatives, the older persons, that is, continue to observe the religious aspects of the event. They fast and attend the services regularly.

The present generation of Ouranoupolis, however, write to Santa for their gifts and have sacks to accommodate the many presents they expect. And yes, they have the Christmas tree, the children finding it difficult to contain their patience to see it erected, helping to decorate it. When all is ready, as children everywhere, they ask, "How many more sleeps to Christmas Day, Mummy?"

This was not so in my childhood. On the first day of Christmas, after the Liturgy, the children, in groups of threes and fours, would go around the village singing our Greek equivalent of carols: Christ is born today in the city of Bethlehem, the Heavens rejoice, all Creation is jubilant! But their reward would have been simply a handful of dried figs or almonds, whatever was in the house. From the homes of the rich, a drachma, perhaps.

We were always glad to have Christmas over and done with. We looked forward eagerly to December 31 instead. New Year's Eve is a time when all the family gather round the table. The children listen for the bells, which announce the arrival of Ayios Vassilios. He comes from far away Caesarea in a magnificent carriage pulled by white horses. We were assured of this by our parents, but we never actually met him. However, we knew that he had come to our house during the night because there were a few

146

nuts and dry figs left behind for us.

New Year's Eve would bring lots of things to eat. No presents were thought of back in that time, and we expected none. It was Vassilopita (so named in honour of Ayios Vassilios), we longed for: the delicious pie with the floori–the golden coin–like the silver six pence in the Christmas pudding. In those days, it was a drachma; more than one had to be strategically placed to prevent disappointing all the siblings. Vassilopita, a mille feuille pie, is common only to the people who had lived in Asia Minor and carry on the tradition in Greece. In other parts of the country, a simple sponge cake is baked instead.

Grandma spent many hours preparing the paper-thin pastry circles. I can see her even now kneeling by the bread-making trough, one lump of dough the size of a tennis ball in her hands. She had a metre length of doweling the thickness of an adult finger nearby for rolling out the dough. She would then begin by placing the dough in the centre of the base of the trough, put the rolling pin right across it and begin to make a circular shape by continually moving it round and round whilst rolling it, dusting the circle with flour to stop it from sticking to the rolling pin. The circles of pastry had the diameter of the baking tin; it could be whatever container was available up to twenty-six centimetres. Grandma would produce half a dozen or more of these and lay them out on flat surfaces like beds and tables to dry enough so they would not collapse when handled.

In the meantime, sugar and mixed spice with ground blanched almonds were pounded together. The aroma was exquisite! The tapsi (dish) would be thoroughly oiled; the golden coin (a drachma wrapped in oiled paper) was the first object to grace the tapsi. Then, as each layer was placed a spoonful of the pounded mixture was spread evenly over its entire surface until all were used. The top layer was left blank to be decorated with split-blanched almonds. It was up to the person who made the Vassilopita to choose a design. It was almost the same in every household: the Year date and Good Wishes. After baking, and while still warm, a cup of syrup was poured over it, which was what made the Vassilopita so delicious!

The ritual of cutting and dividing the Vassilopita had to be undertaken only by the head of the family: the father. Sitting at the head of the table, he would cross himself and ask for God's blessing on those present and also for the absent ones. Our father would pick up the knife and make the sign of the cross over the mouth-watering Vassilopita. The first wedge was dedicated to The Panagia (the All Holy One); the next one to Jesus; then to family members, according to seniority in the household—Father, Mamma, Grandma, St. Basil (Ayios Vassilios) until all present were allocated a slice.

Lifting the first slice is a moment of holding our breath because no child wants the Mother of God to find the floori. Continuing with the next slice and the next, no floori is found! The next is for one of our twin sisters—yes! As father turns the slice over, we see the little parcel sure enough; one of the children was indeed the lucky one.

"Look under the rest of the slices, please!" implore our little brothers, and as if by miracle, the last slice for the youngest brother has a parcel. He has a floori also!

All is well now. Before we go to bed, Mamma slides a slice of Vassilopita onto a plate, pours a little home-grown wine in a small glass and hands it to our father, who places both items on the high shelf in the bedroom, where the bread is kept under a cloth. Ayios Vassilios will come in the small hours; he will drink the wine and eat his portion of the Vassilopita. He will visit us again hopefully next year to receive his offering.

Two incidents come to mind as I recount the New Year celebrations. The table was set for the special meal of chicken and pilaf of couscous. The Vassilopita was brought out from its secret place. This was in order to keep little fingers from picking the decorations. We were waiting for our patera (father) to come home from the taverna to start the meal. It was nearing midnight and he was still absent. All became restless and disappointed; our little brothers began to whimper and like the rest of us, they were hungry and dispirited. Mamma decided to send me and my sister Angeliki to bring our father home. Evgenia, her twin, remained at home to help amuse the boys with stories.

The taverna was only two blocks away, but it was a dark night. We looked at the dim lights of the houses to find our way. We arrived chilled and scared of his reception. He was very annoyed with us for disturbing his card game and ordered us home. Our poor mother did her best to reassure us that he would be on time to begin the meal and cut the pita. But we had to go and call him again. This time we stood beside him at the card table and would not return home without him. The homecoming was not a happy one that year.

I cannot recollect how old I was when my faith was destroyed, nor can I remember why I was with my paternal grandparents on that particular New Year. It was nearing midnight and round the table were Grandmother Annika, Grandfather Yiannis, Aunt Olga and myself. The chicken pilaf was served; we ate and listened for the carriage bells announcing the arrival of Ayios Vassilios. They sounded very close and so very loud. No wonder: I looked across the table at my grandfather, whose hands were under the table and his arms moving rapidly! As I slid down from my chair, I glimpsed something shiny. The polished pestle and mortar in granddad's hands—only another child who is told that Father Christmas doesn't exist will appreciate my feelings at the revelation.

"Oh, no! Is there no Agios Vassilios who comes every year? Granddad, why did you let me find out otherwise?"

The following years had no magic for me. Poor Grandfather—he was so very upset for destroying my belief in that person who came from a faraway country in a carriage full of little bags with nuts and figs for all the children in our world—our cosmos, our village. We knew of no other habitation.

THE RETURN

I longed for the return of my godparents.

It happened like this: It was my job to take our two goats to the herdsman each morning and bring them home on their return. Despite the all-day feeding, they always returned hungry and were reluctant to be led home. It was on one such occasion, the sun had already gone home, and I had left the house to collect our goats, Bijou and Pipitsou. On the way I passed a friend, she was my age, sitting on the front doorstep of her home. She looked extremely thin and yellow. I did feel sorry for her. She was another malaria victim like myself.

I joined the group waiting for the animals to arrive. We saw three men approach in the distance: a tall one between two short ones. One of the short men was familiar to me, as he was the postman we shared with many other villages. He was unique in that he was the only constant outsider who came to our world. The other short man was a stranger to us. And the man in the centre wore a long military coat—who was he?

Oh! There, before my very eyes, materialised my long-gone and longed-for godfather! It was like a dream come true, for I often saw him in my sleep, but he was always gone on waking up. This time, however, it was for real!

But what a sight I must have looked after my recent bout of malaria. He swooped down, picked me up as if I were as light as a rag doll and said, "Sydnoula mou posso se agapo my little Sydney—I love you so much!"

He spent two days in the village, but before he departed, he promised to give me the opportunity to attend school in Thessaloniki. After three days, the travellers sailed away in a rowing boat to the pick-up point at Trypiti, near Xerxes's canal. My godfather requested that I go with him that far. I sat very close to him. I remember feeling seasick and rested my head on his lap: I wonder whether he detected the nits on my long hair? They were only empty cells by then; the lice had long emerged and had been removed by Mamma. The empty cells were simply too well cemented to be removed by washing and combing, each nit had to be handpicked for complete removal.

My godparents became the saviours of our village by providing many amenities through their writing. Water was piped to a tap in the main crossroads, agricultural tools were made available, Chios sheep—which produced high yields of milk and fleece—were given to those who could breed them so that more people would benefit. A prefabricated school building was another much-needed facility, and so was a wooden church, even though there was already a chapel in the Tower, less frequently used after the earthquake.

The Lochs conceived the idea to facilitate and achieve education for village girls aged fourteen to sixteen years, whose schooling had been interrupted by the Second World War. They hoped this would make up for the total absence of learning during the war years. The school's name was The Quaker Home Economics School for Girls. The aim was to educate and train future housewives. The plan was to invite forty girls from surrounding villages, mostly in Halkidiki. The indefatigable Joice and Sydney Loch set off in their jeep and began a recruiting campaign visiting those villages and giving parents the opportunity to allow their young daughters to join the school. Most parents embraced the offer; very few turned it down.

The school was about two kilometres from the American Farm School for boys. Theirs was a school built with bricks and stones; the girls' school was simply two wooden barracks that had been occupied by German officers during the invasion of Greece. The Quaker school was sponsored by the Quakers and some other kind people from the United Kingdom; may I offer my thanks to all the persons who assisted in the establishment and maintenance of the school—it was a giant step into a better future for all of us.

My entry to the Quaker school was scheduled for October. My godfather explained that the curriculum would include more

151

subjects that the State schools could match. English was to be taught by an actual English teacher—a Quaker, Hilda Davies. Greek teachers would teach Cooking, Dressmaking, Agriculture, Silkworm Management, Baby Care—and to our astonishment and delight—folk singing and dancing. We never had it so good! We embraced all of the above, plus Greek and Greek language, Religious Knowledge, History, Geography and Mathematics. It was an imaginative and inspiring curriculum compiled by the Greek principal, Miss Avrilia Vachou (also a Quaker), and three female teachers fresh from University. They were young, beautiful and very kind to us. We came to love them; only two are still alive now. I met up with them recently in Greece. The reunion was extremely emotional. Teachers and students had become unrecognisable, as the years had left their marks on our faces and on our bodies.

Miss Nanda was the artist who designed the border of the school certificate. She was petite and athletic; she taught art, Greek, Greek language and dressmaking. She now has a summer house near my village in Nea Rhoda. I hope to meet up with her again this year. Miss Katerina taught Mathematics, Geography and History. I remembered her as a tall person, but she became short and frail over the years. Her beautiful black hair that once hung in shiny ringlets was a ghost of its former self. Miss Katy had been very tall and willowy. Her long light brown hair was always restrained in two glossy plaits. She had been engaged to a handsome young man with a monster of a black motor bike. The noisy engine announced its arrival long before it was sighted. Miss Katy was the agriculturalist; sadly, she is no longer with us.

Religious Knowledge was the principal's cherished subject. Miss Avrilia Vlachou, the school principal was a middle-aged woman. Of medium height, she had a full figure and wore her grey hair like pear-shaped earmuffs. Although friendly and cheerful, she commanded respect and authority. Strangely, she could discipline by actually promoting the offender. For example, Dora was one of the sixteen-year-old students. She was boisterous, noisy and had a colourful vocabulary. She was a bully; we had suffered in silence long enough and one day decided to report her to Miss Vlachou.

The matter was taken in hand immediately: Dora was summoned. We expected and hoped the punishment would be severe. We wanted our pound of flesh. Instead, a smiling Dora, head held high, joined us in the study and announced that from now on she was in charge of discipline: she would tolerate no bad behaviour so we had better look out! She became a model of good behaviour herself as a result. A lesson for the rest of us and one I make use of to this day.

Miss Vlachou was a very patient teacher. We didn't know that the Bible was in two parts: The New and Old Testaments. We could not recite the Lord's Prayer or the Holy Creed. "Shame on you!" declared my Godmother scornfully. I was certain that I could never learn the Lord's Prayer and the Creed by heart. Both looked difficult and lengthy. However, I eventually succeeded, thanks to Miss Vlachou's encouragement. Indeed, in order to demonstrate my eagerness to learn and to reassure my godparents that I meant to work hard, I was set extra homework by the principal: 1 Corinthians, Chapter 13. I have no recollection how many times I read and reread it until I succeeded and recited it in the presence of my Godparents, the teachers and my fellow pupils.

At Easter, we were given a prayer book called Synopsis. It was signed and dated by: Mr. and Mrs. Sydney Loch, Miss Vlachou and the teachers. It is still in my possession, a little worse for wear. It contains the Easter services, including the dates for Easter from 1916 to 2000. In 1948, it was on May 2nd and in 1983, it was May 8th.

I enjoyed my two years at that school. I learnt what I missed in primary school and much more besides. Many of the students went on to further education but most returned home, married and produced their own families. My godfather was anxious to provide for my future career and was determined that I should continue with further education. He decided that Kalamari, the French convent and a private school for girls in Thessaloniki, would be the best school for me to attend. There I would learn the French language and possibly a little English, which was taught once a week. French lessons were every day, and French was to be spoken by the boarders in the presence of staff.

At the beginning, I was out of my depth; this was another culture. Day and boarder girls came from rich families. They were sophisticated and their talk was on alien subjects to me. They wore expensive clothes when out of uniform. They boasted of life in luxurious houses and second homes for the summer holidays. I did make friends eventually and settled down to a routine of school and homework. My village was too far to go to during the school year and my godparents were often away. This meant I would be in the convent in the company of the nuns most of the time.

This isolation from my peer groups proved beneficial for my French language, however. I discovered French comics that first summer. I found the simple words easy to understand. That led to reading simple books, followed by many happy hours enjoying French literature and succeeding in obtaining the Certificate of the French Language. That was a long time ago: I speak only fluent English now. On leaving Kalamari, I arrived in England to a new culture and the beginning of my future profession.

In the morning of August 6th, 1950, after affectionate embraces and goodbyes, Iraclis, my father and Sydney Loch, my godfather, watched me climb onto an aircraft bound for Athens. It was an amazing experience to feel airborne after being earthbound for 19 years. The descent into Athens was exhilarating and frightening because it was so rapid and as we were about to touch down, the aircraft vibrated and I trembled with fear.

Within hours, I was again climbing aboard the "Skymaster," the fastest aeroplane in the Olympic fleet, which would bring me to London. The entire flight took 12 hours, stopping for refuelling twice, first in Rome then Paris—a day of excitement and anticipation.

A new life began for me in another country where I would work and study in order to fulfil my godfather's aspirations for me to achieve a profession. To this end, I applied myself and succeeded in obtaining: State Registration in General Nursing, State Certification in Midwifery, Diploma in Orthopaedic Nursing and Qualification in Microbiology.

I enjoyed my working life in various branches of the profession, including assisting in the Matron's office. I was one of the first thirteen nurses in the UK to be appointed to the post of clinical nurse specialist in Infection Control, a position I held until my retirement in 1993.

EXODUS

August 6, 1945–I was fourteen years old and setting out on the greatest adventure of my life. The date is also significant for another reason, for I left Greece for England five years later on that same date. All my belongings were placed in a cloth bag, just as many years later, I would watch with pleasure as my three-year-old granddaughter, Millie, departing for Philadelphia, USA, pulled behind her a small pink case on wheels containing all her own personal items.

Mamma and I left on foot for Nea Rhoda. We were soon caught up with by a distraught Byron, my nine-year-old brother, who insisted on joining us for the long trek to our destination. I remember telling him to turn back–I wanted to have Mother all to myself on this journey. It was to no avail: he wept miserably and begged to come with us. Mamma had enough love and room in her heart for both of us.

We walked along the single foot path for most of the first part of the morning: hot dust under foot, a scorching brilliant sun overhead. We came here every year, on August the twenty-fourth, to celebrate the anniversary of the Panagia's passing away. It was a panegiry, a festival, held in a clearing near fields on the way to the village of Nea Rhoda. It was the highlight of the summer. We didn't mind the long trek from our village, even though we walked barefoot. The icon of the Holy Virgin was carried here; a short service would take place followed by a few women who sat on the ground and took the icon in turn on their lap. At that moment, there would be a spectacle that had to be seen to be believed. The icon would begin to hit the woman on the head. I was there; I saw it. Was it the trembling hands of the so-called sinners who were terrified of the Virgin's wrath, or was the miraculous icon truly punishing the guilty? We, the children, were too happy going to the various stalls looking at trifles and trinkets to be concerned about the religious events of the festival or their meaning.

On this particular day, we were walking along on the way to Nea Rhoda when Mamma drew our attention to a bird. She said it was a hawk. It seemed suspended over the vineyard.

"Watch children!" she said.

The bird flew down and came up into the clear sky with a snake dangling from its beak.

"How could the hawk have seen it from that height?" we inquired.

"It has excellent eye sight, much better than ours," was her reply.

We pressed on, arriving at Aunt Maria's. By then, we were sweaty, dusty, thirsty and exhausted. I don't remember much of the rest of that day, only the talk among the adults about preparations for the voyage to Stavros: a small seaside town with a fishing industry and a train service to Thessaloniki, which was my ultimate goal.

Only now that I am a mother myself do I appreciate how painful it must have been for my mother to return home without me. When my first daughter left home for university, she was eighteen years old and much-travelled with and without the family. The only places I had been to at that young age were the island of Ammouliani and Nea Rhoda.

My own daughter's departure left me bereft. I kept her photograph on my bedside table. But I was able to visit and telephoned her often, whereas Mamma was forced to let me go to an uncertain future for my education. She was not able to communicate with me except by letter, and she did not have my photograph. I didn't see my family again for a year. Of course, homesickness engulfed me and was my companion until my godfather came back into my life for the second time. I have no recollection of parting from Mamma and Byron. I suspect there were many tears shed and lots of clinging hugs. At the time, however, I was focussed only on my adventure.

The party to Stavros consisted of seven persons: Aunt Maria and Photis her husband; Yiannis and Cotsos, her brothers; Piyi and Phopho, her teenage nieces; and myself. We embarked soon after sunrise onto a small rowing boat with an outboard motor. I cannot remember what clothes we wore except for Phopho, who wore a pink slip with shoulder straps. But I do remember the sight of my own legs sitting on the triangular part at the front of the boat, stretched out like bamboo canes. I hadn't realised before how thin I was, because I fancied myself rather a well-developed grown-up, even though I had yet to begin menstruating and was hopelessly flat-chested.

We chugged along very slowly because the men were looking out for fish to dynamite. The idea was to get a big catch and sell it upon arrival at Stavros. It was an unforgettable experience for me. When the dynamite hit the water, the clear blue sea became churned up and frothy. As it cleared, dead fish floated to the surface. We remained stationary for a little while, bobbing up and down gently, while the fish were gathered up. We watched Phopho dive: I can see her now—her slip filled up and billowed as if by the wind, showing off her white knickers. I was anxious about her safety as she swam so near the dynamite detonations.

Although the distance was only 9.5 miles, it took the entire day to reach Olympiada, the island between us and Stavros. The four adults took up their musical instruments and the serenade began. Aunt Maria strummed on the guitar and sang, Photis played his violin, the two brothers blew on wind instruments and the nieces joined in the singing. It was a cheerful and joyful trip. I am ashamed to admit that I didn't think of the family I left behind, not even my mother. I was seduced by the prospect of a happy future and felt it had already begun on the little boat. Little could I have imagined what awaited me.

Yiannis and Cotsos rolled their trouser legs up and jumped in the sea just as we were about to run aground on Olympiada. They pulled the boat halfway up the shore. We jumped onto dry, hot sand and pebbles and settled down to a feast of freshly caught and fish cooked on a fire by the shore. The men drank ouzo during the cooking process while picking at the fish. We devoured the meal of white fleshy catch, smelling and tasting of the sea. We tore pieces with our fingers and licked them clean. They washed down the repast with home-brewed wine. The men did the cooking. Usually the women washed up, but after such a meal, there were no dishes to wash, only our hands, which were soon rinsed in the warm sea.

Piyitsa–the diminutive name of Piyi–she was older than Phopho, her sister, and many years my senior. She suggested we watched the sunset. She told us that, as the sun goes down behind the island, it looks like a champagne glass. As I had no idea what such an object looked like, I could show little enthusiasm, but Phopho was thrilled with the apparition for some reason.

We dug our beds out of the warm sand and bedded down in a straight row. The adults began telling anecdotes, which caused a lot of hilarity. Piyitsa and Phopho found them funny also. I saw nothing to laugh about. They were very naughty rhymes with double meanings! I remember them clearly even now, because I repeated them so many times and eventually came to understand what they meant, with a little explanation from Phopho.

Another day at sea in warm sunshine scorched us. We arrived in Stavros at dusk. Here we parted company with our fellow mariners; only Aunt Maria and I remained together. That night was simply punishing–we had to sleep on the bare floor, which felt cold and hard. Sleep evaded us. Tossing and turning hurt our thin and thinly clad bodies. Our bedfellows were bedbugs and cockroaches. They attacked us ferociously; scratching to relieve the itchiness made little difference. We prayed for the light of dawn when our torturers would depart.

I don't remember where we washed or whether we had anything to eat; however, I do recollect Aunt Maria taking me for a stroll along the beach where there were many big boats, partly destroyed, lining the shore. It was ghostly and sad: an unforgettable sight. She explained to me it was the aftermath of the Second World War.

How did we fill that day? All I remember now is my impatience to leave for Thessaloniki and be united with my godparents who would be pleased to see me, or so I believed. Little did I know of the reception awaiting me.

We set off in the cool of the evening to get the train. The

railway lines were level with the platform. Waiting seemed interminable: what if the train failed to arrive? Aunt Maria reassured me that it would come soon.

Suddenly, a roar assailed our ears. I tightened my grip on Aunt Maria and trembled with fear at the approaching noise: a big round light accompanied the ugly roar, and it was coming right towards us! I could hardly stand up straight, it was such a monster. I didn't notice that no one else was in the same fearful state as I was.

"Here is our train," announced Aunty, trying to reassure me.

In spite of my fourteen years, I had never travelled far from my small village. I didn't know what a train looked like or the noise it made. The train took us on board, offering hard wooden seats for us to sit on.

The monotonous noise sent us to sleep as we sat huddled together for comfort and support. I remember little of that overnight journey: sleep took care of that. But I do recollect holding Aunt Maria's hand firmly and greeting every person we came across.

"My child you don't greet people who are strangers. This is Thessaloniki; it is not your village where you know and are known by everybody," whispered Aunty. We were en route to the British Embassy to meet my godmother, Joice Loch, so that I could be handed over to her.

I was overwhelmed by the traffic. It was noisy; the buildings looked very tall, the roads wide and full of people. The Embassy was a long way from the railway station. We walked on for ages to reach it and when we actually made it, we settled down on the steps near the entrance to wait for my godmother. Aunty instructed me to approach the unsuspecting Joice Loch when she was level with us: "Take her hand and kiss it." This is a sign of respect in Greece.

My godmother finally appeared and climbed the steps rather slowly. When she was on the same step, I rushed forward, grabbed her hand and kissed it as instructed. She withdrew it in horror. She was furious—the look on her face was thunderous. I was shocked and frightened by her obvious repulsion. I couldn't understand what she was saying because I spoke no English then, but understood by her manner that she was not at all pleased to see me. Her Greek was limited, but I heard her say "perimeni," meaning, "wait." I stood with Aunty and waited for my godmother to return. She came out of the Embassy eventually, spoke to Aunt Maria, who then took her leave, and motioned me to follow her into her chauffeur-driven car.

In hindsight, I now understand her unkind reaction at my intrusion into her life: she had been given no idea of my arrival in town. She was busy with the Quaker Relief Service, as I have already described to you. She was simply unprepared to handle both me and her very important work.

The car fascinated me; it seemed to drive itself. It differed so much from the carts drawn by oxen. We sped out of town towards the country to the American Farm School, where my godparents lived on their return from Quaker Relief Service in the spring of 1945. It was a silent journey; my godmother remained unforgiving. I was intimidated and shocked by her attitude but comforted myself with the expectation of an affectionate reunion with my beloved godfather. I imagined there would be a little room in their house for me and that life would continue where it left off in 1938.

The car pulled up by a summer camp for orphans, normally resident in a Thessaloniki orphanage. The orphans had arrived that day to spend two weeks at the camp. On their return, another group would have the same opportunity to enjoy normality in the fresh air. But, before the morrow, they would have to undergo cleansing by hand and autoclave. This was the same experience awaiting me. I remember even now my great disappointment that day. I felt I was being punished for my very existence. No sign of my godfather—was he told that I had been dumped at the summer camp?

He arrived late that afternoon, after our trip to Thessaloniki, where we were taken in an open lorry to be disinfected, deloused and for all our belongings to be autoclaved. I had a white dress, which opened from neck to well below the waist. It fastened with enormous buttons: it had been remodelled from an adult garment to fit me for my new life. I was told to make it into a sack for my property. With sadness, I tied the sleeves together, turned the dress into a bag, and put my few belongings in it. I was asked to remove everything except knickers and petticoat. Of course, I complied, feeling utterly humiliated. I added the rest of my smalls into the bag and handed it to a woman who wore white overalls, her head covered in a white cloth to protect her from infestation. My property joined that of my fellows in the autoclave, to be sterilised so that no lice or nits would survive.

Worse was to come. This ghostly clad woman asked to me to come forward. She held an atomiser like the one used by Grandma to spray sulphur powder on the young vine leaves. She pushed the handle; it produced a cloud of white powder directed at my hair, which was long—well below my shoulders—and a light golden brown. The unfortunate female orphans' hair was cut very short, past all dignity. As for the boys' hair, it was shorn most severely. It could not have supported much livestock anyway. The ghastly woman then inserted the atomizer under my petticoat and inside my knickers pumping out more clouds. I was thoroughly dusted with DDT and could taste it in my mouth. My eyes became dry and sore. Mamma would have been devastated to see me in such a state as she had taken great care to ensure my hair was free from lice and nits. Yet in spite of her efforts, here I was being treated like an infested street urchin.

We then were asked to make our way to the back of the autoclave. We collected the sterile clothes and put on our outer garments before we were herded into the lorry like small, subdued animals to return to camp. We slid around on the lorry as before, looking for a hold to stop us from being tossed about like pieces of merchandise. I will never forget that undignified and humiliating experience: it is still vivid in my memory.

My godfather did come to welcome me finally. He was very kind and affectionate, but what he thought of my appearance was not mentioned then or at any other time by him or by me. He took me to the cinema. I remember that upon returning to the camp, I was unable to give a meaningful explanation of the film. It was the first time I had seen and heard actors perform. I had arrived in a completely new world that perplexed and embarrassed me. "The little peasant" must have been the epithet attached to my name.

The other children (the orphans) slept in big rooms in long narrow beds painted blue. I remember young men and women

161

shared those quarters to take care of their charges. As for myself, I was handed over to a teacher, who was asked to look after me. A camp bed was made ready, placed on the opposite side against the wall. A big black dog slept on the floor between us. I woke up in the night confused: I had turned round in my sleep; my head was where my feet should have been. Where was I? Then, as I put my hand out trying to reach the teacher's bed, I touched the dog's head instead and cried out in panic. My companion was at once by my side and reassured me with a much-appreciated hug.

It was easy and effortless to mix with the other children. One toddler was mute; he was often segregated into a room because he was always crying. I peeped into his isolation one day to find him wearing only a vest, the lower part of his body exposed. He was leaning to one side dragging himself along the floor. I had seen nudity before: One of the brothers I left behind in the village was of similar age to this child. What shocked me however was the raw flesh bulging from his anus. Oh the poor little boy! I can now guess the reason for his distress: the bulge was a prolapsed rectum, which was the result of the continuous crying, in order to communicate his needs. He became intolerable to his carers with his almost animal-like cries for attention.

During that summer, I was hospitalised to have my appendix removed. Entering the hospital was a suffocating shock. Such bad smells as I had never come across permeated the air. The familiar village smells from goats, other beasts of burden and the sea breezes were absent here. The hospital smelt simply revolting; there was no other word for it. There were long dark corridors. I glimpsed patients in their beds as we passed by making our way to a surgical ward.

I was eventually seen by two surgeons. I was moved twice to other adult wards, I saw no other children. A beautiful nurse led me to a bathroom, no explanation offered. She picked up a razor and attacked my sparse pubic teenage hair. I was so terribly embarrassed that I avoided her at all times thereafter.

The day of my surgery arrived. I was afraid and wanted to run away, but there was nowhere to go. Only to the surgical theatre, of course! I actually had to walk there—no premedication in those days. Then I climbed on the operating table and had my hands tied to its frame. A man, presumably the anaesthetist, put a thick wad of cotton wool soaked in ether on my face and asked me to count. I did, up to sixteen or seventeen, I think. It didn't take long before I was out for the count.

I came to in a wave of overwhelming nausea: I retched much and often. There was no one to hold my forehead like Mamma always did following the malaria attacks. Here I was alone - feeling sick, my mouth filling up with froth and nothing could alleviate the condition. During visiting times, I hid under the bed covers and had a silent weep. I felt absolutely lonely, abandoned and forgotten by everyone. Within days, the wound felt hot; it hurt: it was infected.

I woke up the next morning with my thighs stuck together. Apparently, an abscess had burst inside me, and the pus acted as glue on my legs. Later in the morning, a doctor and a nurse arrived at my bedside. The doctor explained that it was necessary to drain the wound in order to allow it to heal.

Without warning, he pointed his scalpel down and across the original incision and cut: I screamed with pain.

The wound remained opened for thirty days and left an ugly scar. I was discharged back to the camp with that open wound. Each day, the local doctor—she was a Russian refugee—came to dress it. She used a piece of cotton wool with a few drops of petrol and cleaned the infected site, applied a gauze dressing and departed to return the next day. We had no common language between us: nodding and smiling became our tongue instead. We became friends. She continued to attend to the wound until it healed, a month later.

My godfather came to see me almost every day as before. He took me to the cinema and for walks, which served as coaching classes in the rudiments of the English language. He was very patient, kind and affectionate. This was a great comfort during the seven weeks I remained in the camp. In October, I joined thirty-nine girls at the Quaker School and stayed there for two years.

DEATH LAID OUT

The master bedroom of our family home as I mentioned before was a place for much sorrow. Though it had witnessed such joys as the birth of children and the love of my mother and father, it had also been a place that witnessed the death of loved ones.

It was in the mid-thirties when my maternal Grandfather lay dead on a low bed in the middle of the master bedroom. He was fully dressed in his best clothes, with shoes on his feet. His arms were crossed over his chest; an icon was resting against his hands.

I remember my Grandmother dressed in black with a black scarf covering her hair, kneeling beside her husband, sobbing. It was the first time that I ever saw my Grandma in such distress. My Mother and her two sisters were also in black and in tears. To me, he simply looked asleep. I was four years old at the time. It seemed that day as if the entire population of our village passed through our house. People would arrive throughout the day carrying flowers. They knelt beside my grandfather, made the sign of the cross, kissed the icon, his forehead and then arranged the flowers round and on top of him.

My family had relatives in Ammoliani, the island that lay opposite the village. Someone must have taken a rowing boat over to the island to break the sad news and to bring them to the house. They all arrived dressed in black, also carrying flowers. They knelt, crossed themselves, kissed the icon, the forehead, crying and talking to him. He never spoke back to them. With white handkerchiefs trimmed in black, they wiped their many tears. I was an observer almost to the end because it was the first time that I had been exposed to death but I could not have understood its finality at such a young age.

The church bell began to toll and everyone started to cry loudly. A coffin was brought into the room, my Grandfather was lifted into and carried to the church by four young men. The priest, also in black, stood in front of the temple and the service began. Meanwhile, the assembled family, relatives and the entire village populace thronged round the coffin, some crying audibly, others sobbing softly to themselves. A very long service was followed by an even longer procession to the cemetery. It was there in that place where realisation dawned on me. I squeezed between those gathered obstructing my view and came to a big hole into which my grandfather was being lowered. It was then that I knew what it meant to be dead.

I would never see him again.

Never again would he hold me in his arms.

I sobbed my heart out. Gentle hands dragged me away; a young woman picked me up and held me to her tightly: Her name was Aphroditi. As we rejoined the procession home, she tried to comfort me telling me that my Grandfather had gone to Constantinople, and on his return would bring me a golden bracelet. But that made me all the more upset. How could she tell such an untruth? All I knew was that my Grandfather was in the grave and the priest threw a spade full of earth on the coffin where he lay.

After the burial it is traditional to offer to each person there koliva—wheat soaked overnight, boiled the next day, then mixed with sugar and spices. It is customarily given with a soft, sweet bun. After the service the families will gather with relatives and friends at one of the tavernas for coffee and brandy. However, this tends only to prolong the distress and the pressing sense of loss at a time when most bereaved families need to be at home to mourn in private.

On the 5th of October 1968, it was in that same place that an unexpected tragedy struck: Our beloved mother died at only sixty-two years of age. By then I was living happily in England a long way away with my young family. I was completely unaware of her passing and received a letter from Joice Loch, my godmother, two weeks later to inform me of our sad loss. It was the late sixties, yet even then the village was still cut off from the rest of the world. I

165

could speak to no other family members, neither to console nor mourn with them. I felt so isolated and engulfed by abject misery and guilt, for being so far away from home.

Again, on the 6th of August 2005, this same chamber bore witness to the suffering and death of our beautiful sister, Angeliki, who up until then had been such an active and healthy woman. An enthusiastic gardener, a regular walker and swimmer up to nine months every year prior to her untimely death, she was just seventy-two years old. Evgenia, her twin, died at the age of nineteen, away from home in Thessaloniki and was buried near there at the American Farm School for Boys. Our sister had been a student at the Quaker school for Girls nearby.

MODERNISATION

The image of the village has changed almost beyond recognition. Most of the old houses were razed to the ground and new dwellings allowed to spring up all higgledy-piggledy. Some rose to three stories high, others were built one story at a time so that the village became a series of flat rooftops, displaying washing lines festooned with billowing clothes, television aerials, and vines supported on horizontal frames. A few years ago, I saw an uncle climb to the flat roof of my brother's house. He actually pegged there about a dozen filleted mackerel to be cured by the sun. But within minutes, maybe half an hour, a raucous noise announced the arrival of seagulls swooping down on the fish and devouring the lot in minutes and then flying away. It was fortunate that I had witnessed the episode, because Uncle Vassili was bound to accuse my sister-in-law: Relations between them were often inflammatory.

My Godmother, Joice Loch, watched the changes and warned that the people would change for the worse. She prophesied accurately; brother turned against brother over the share of inheritance, so resistant to all amicable solutions that they'd end up in court, spending all their savings and creating enmity and widespread division, where once there had been affection and amity.

Modernisation, however, wasn't always for the worse. The village needed roads in order to communicate and interact with other human beings. New blood was in short supply, as most of us seemed to be related to each other. The village population has greatly swelled to well over 600 hundred out of season, and–during the summer–beyond counting due to the visitors.

The road certainly brought a much-needed doctor. He visited

and still continues to do so once a week, usually on Thursday. A doctor is essential, though the delegated medical man is customarily very young and newly qualified. He is sent to remote villages to gain experience and solve the numerous medical problems. Indeed, he probably learns much from his patients.

But in the summer of 2007, a second doctor arrived. I saw a notice in three languages (English, German and Russian, reflecting the potential patients' origins, no doubt), and when I enquired of the person on the premises just who this additional doctor could be, I learned he, himself was a young Russian who, having studied medicine in Greece, had set up a temporary private practice and hoped to be of assistance to the numerous tourists.

Tourism was necessary: it was the lesser of two evils. It was good for the economy; people soon embraced the tourist trade with great enthusiasm. Shops sprang up selling once undreamed of merchandise for the benefit of the tourists but also much appreciated by the permanent residents.

The village became very noisy and crowded; but how much better than the people having to eke out a living working in the fields in all weathers without proper agricultural tools, or , most of them going to work on Athos away from their families? In the old days working on Athos would leave whole families fatherless for weeks, forcing the womenfolk to take to the fields to be in charge of harvesting the wheat and the grapes, wine making, gathering the olives, taking them to the olive press, all in that order. Not that every family owned three such properties, but the old times were hard; the new way of earning a living is less arduous and more rewarding.

The roads are now surfaced with tarmac. The dust in the summer and mud in the winter are no longer problems. Now a bigger problem has developed: the arrival of the automobile. It seemed as if every household suddenly owned its own vehicle and parked it proudly outside their home. And of course, the Thessalonians and Athenians would arrive in cars adding to the congestion.

In the shadow of the Tower there is a square. In the old days it was an open space for any person to pass the time of day sitting on the bench gazing out at sea its traffic and the sun going home behind the island of Ammouliani.. I had my wedding reception in the square. My father, armed with a tray, brandy and glasses, and accompanied by three musicians, went from house to house and invited everyone to attend. The church was full. After the service, all the guests spilled out, pouring into the square to celebrate with food and wine and dancing, well into the small hours. The old square has maintained some of its old communal purpose in these modern times—as the venue for the midnight Easter service for one. The church and the area immediately surrounding it no longer have the capacity to accommodate everyone who wishes to attend: the parishioners, the visiting Greeks who come expressly for that ceremony, and the tourists who show their appreciation by observing silence, unlike most of the Greek visitors and my compatriots.

There are four buses daily. They start in Thessaloniki and most of the passengers head for the villages along the route. By the time they reach Trypiti, the penultimate stop before the terminus in Ouranoupolis; it fills up again with the tourists who stay in the hotels along the coast. The bus disgorges them into Tower Square; all are interested in the local food, the souvenirs, and the cruise to Mount Athos to see all the monasteries without setting foot on its holy soil. Visitors from Sithonia, the middle finger of Halkidiki, sail to the village to have lunch and leave in the afternoon to admire the Athos monasteries from the deck of their cruiser.

In the old days of my youth, our village boasted one hundred bungalows and about four hundred and fifty inhabitants. After my departure at the age of fourteen, and subsequently from the motherland itself, I often found myself homesick at night and discovered much comfort in visiting each household, naming every family member, counting heads more than once, before sleep enfolded me in its embrace and tantalised me with dreams of the village, all who once lived in it and spoke to me. The heavy door for entry to the Tower would be bolted; no one was living inside any more.

Some things do not change. In my dreams tonight, I will, as I did in my tender teenage years, visit the ghosts of my village to ease the ache in my heart. I will visit those people I loved, who are now long gone: Evgenia, her twin Angeliki, Mamma, Father, Grandma and the Lochs. Together, we will whisper of times long past that I keep in my heart and now pass on to you.

Το τέλος

(The End)

For more information about Sydney, maps of her childhood home, and a family tree, please visit www.sydneymwhite.com

Made in the USA
Lexington, KY
17 August 2012